Walks In & Around
BLAENAU
FFESTINIOG

Michael Burnett

KITTIWAKE

Introduction

Until the mid-18thC Blaenau Ffestiniog was the name of an area of remote mountain land in the old parish of Ffestiniog, where there were some farms and sheep-walks but little else of significance. However, when Diffwys Quarry, the first large slate working in the locality, was opened there during the 1760s, it soon became apparent that these uplands, after being quarried and mined, were capable of satisfying an increasing, world-wide, demand for slate. Indeed, in order to service the fast-growing number of quarries, it would soon be necessary to build a town high in the mountains above the Vale of Ffestiniog, to be called Blaenau Ffestiniog. By 1836 the need to transport the roofing slates, and other products of Blaenau's burgeoning industry, resulted in the town becoming connected to Porthmadog by the Ffestiniog Railway; and by 1883 the London and North-Western, and Great Western, railways had opened stations in the town, which continued to expand until the turn of the 20thC. Subsequently the slate industry gradually declined and most quarries closed, leaving only one or two workings in operation during 2017.

Today, evidence of Blaenau Ffestiniog's involvement in the slate industry is inescapable: the awe-inspiring spoil-heaps, decaying inclines, drum-houses and tramways, the derelict quarry buildings, and the old tracks and paths used to get to the quarries by the workers, and into town by their families. Districts of the town, Maenofferen for example, were named after the farms of pre-quarry days, and the terraces of houses built for the quarry workers, and some of their many chapels, have survived. The Ffestiniog Railway and Llechwedd Quarry have been re-born as attractions suited to the needs of 21stC visitors. All of which, together with its wonderful mountain scenery, makes Blaenau Ffestiniog, and its neighbourhood, a fascinating place to visit. And what better way to explore the area than by using the local footways, many now preserved as rights-of-way in recognition of their use by past generations of Blaenau Ffestiniog townspeople?

The twenty walks in this book are aimed at those who arrive in the area by train, bus or car, intending to spend a few hours on a walk, rather than a whole day. The walks vary between 1½ and 4½ miles in length, and introduce visitors to places they would otherwise be unlikely to find during a short visit: minor paths in the town leading to unexpected viewpoints; rights-of-way past magnificent waterfalls; tracks which follow old tramways past mountain lakes; historic settlements, including one high on Manod Mawr; the precipitous gorges of the Cynfal and Teigl rivers.

Information is provided on getting to Blaenau Ffestiniog by bus and train, and the neighbouring villages of Tanygrisiau and Llan Ffestiniog, by connecting buses. For car-drivers, directions to Blaenau Ffestiniog, Tanygrisiau and Llan Ffestiniog from nearby towns are provided, as are details of parking places convenient for the starting points of the walks.

These vary in length and level of difficulty but can all be undertaken by a reasonably fit person. Two of the walks are particularly suitable for families with children. Walking boots or strong shoes, and waterproof clothing, are recommended for all of them. The location of each route is shown on the back cover and a summary of the main characteristics, and approximate length, of each is shown on a chart. An estimated duration is also given but it is best to allow longer in order to linger over the many fine views and interesting places visited whilst on the walks. Each walk has a map and description which enables the route to be followed without further help. However, remember to take account of weather conditions before starting out. A weather forecast for this area is available on 0370 900 0100 (charge) or at www.metoffice.gov.uk.

Enjoy your walks!

Michael Burnett would like to thank the following for their advice and support in the preparation of this book:
The Public Rights of Way Unit at Gwynedd Council, Dolgellau;
Elin Angharad, at Siop Lyfrau'r Hen Bost, 45 High Street, Blaenau Ffestiniog, a bookshop which stocks local guides and maps; and
Cyngor Tref Ffestiniog.

WALK 1
LLYN DUBACH & CAE CLYD

DESCRIPTION This 4½ mile walk explores the wild mountain landscape above Blaenau Ffestiniog. It visits remote lakes and passes disused inclines once integral to Blaenau's world-famous slate industry. Allow 4½ hours.

START The square (SH702458) adjoining the Blaenau Ffestiniog railway station and bus terminal, recently named Sgwar Rawson/Rawson Square.

DIRECTIONS Blaenau Ffestiniog can be reached from Dolgellau via the A470, Porthmadog via the A487/A496 and Betws y Coed via the A5/A470. Park in the car-park near the town-centre and Rawson Square.

BUS & TRAIN SERVICES Buses 35 (from Dolgellau), 1B (from Porthmadog), X1 (from Llandudno and Betws y Coed) and 37 (the Clipa Blaenau local bus) serve Blaenau Ffestiniog. All buses stop in Rawson Square. The railway station adjoins Rawson Square. It is served by mainline trains from Llandudno and Betws y Coed, and by Ffestiniog Railway trains from Porthmadog.

1 Walk out of Rawson Square past the Ty Gorsaf hotel. Turn RIGHT into Stryd Fawr/High Street and walk to Y Meirion pub. Turn LEFT over the nearby pedestrian crossing, then RIGHT past a bus-stop and across Lord Street. Take the next LEFT and walk RIGHT uphill past a waymark. At Brynawel house bear LEFT uphill, then RIGHT between houses. At a junction go LEFT past a waymark and through a wooden gate. Walk uphill on a grassy path and through a metal gate. Go HALF-RIGHT, soon crossing a stream. Then bear RIGHT to another metal gate. *Look back here for a view over Blaenau Ffestiniog to the Moelwyn mountains.*

2 Go through the gate and turn LEFT. Go RIGHT through a metal gate uphill towards some trees. Turn LEFT up a grassy slope opposite an old stone gate pillar. Walk to a fence and waymark. Go RIGHT, initially alongside the fence, then a stream. Bear RIGHT then LEFT onto a track going uphill. Just before the ground levels off, go through a low wall. Then follow the line of the track to a junction of paths.

3 Go RIGHT at the junction then RIGHT when the path divides again soon afterwards. Here the main path goes left and you follow a less distinct path which soon bears LEFT towards a spoil-heap (ignore the path going ahead here). Go RIGHT alongside the foot of the spoil-heap and uphill, bearing LEFT at a junction. Bear RIGHT away from the spoil-heap, passing a low hill beneath the next spoil-heap. Continue AHEAD then across a stream. Continue uphill on the RIGHT of the stream, walk over several boulders and continue to a fence and waymarked post. Cross the stile here and walk LEFT, then bear RIGHT as the path climbs away from the fence to the end of a low ridge. Cross a disused water-channel then walk over the ridge and downhill to a stream. *To the left here is Llyn Dubach and the remains of a dam.*

4 Bear RIGHT away from the stream. Follow the path over the ends of more low ridges and, when you see a wall, go RIGHT through a waymarked gap in it. Walk downhill and cross two streams. Go RIGHT when the path divides, above a reservoir and near a wooden post. Walk downhill, then across a dam. Go LEFT onto a track coming in from the right. *To the right here is an incline which descends steeply to Blaenau Ffestiniog.*

5 Continue along the track *(note the incline from the ridge of Manod Mawr on the left)* following it LEFT uphill near a second reservoir. Continue RIGHT alongside a fence towards Llyn y Manod. Ignore a kissing-gate on the right and walk to the LEFT of the lake. Pass two metal gates then follow a path to the LEFT of the now boggy track. At the end of the lake walk AHEAD uphill, ignoring a path going right to a gate. Bear RIGHT at a junction and make for a fence. *There are good views here south over the Cynfal Valley (see Walks 17 and 18) to Llan Ffestiniog and the Rhinog mountains.* Walk LEFT downhill alongside the fence. Go through a metal

WALK 1

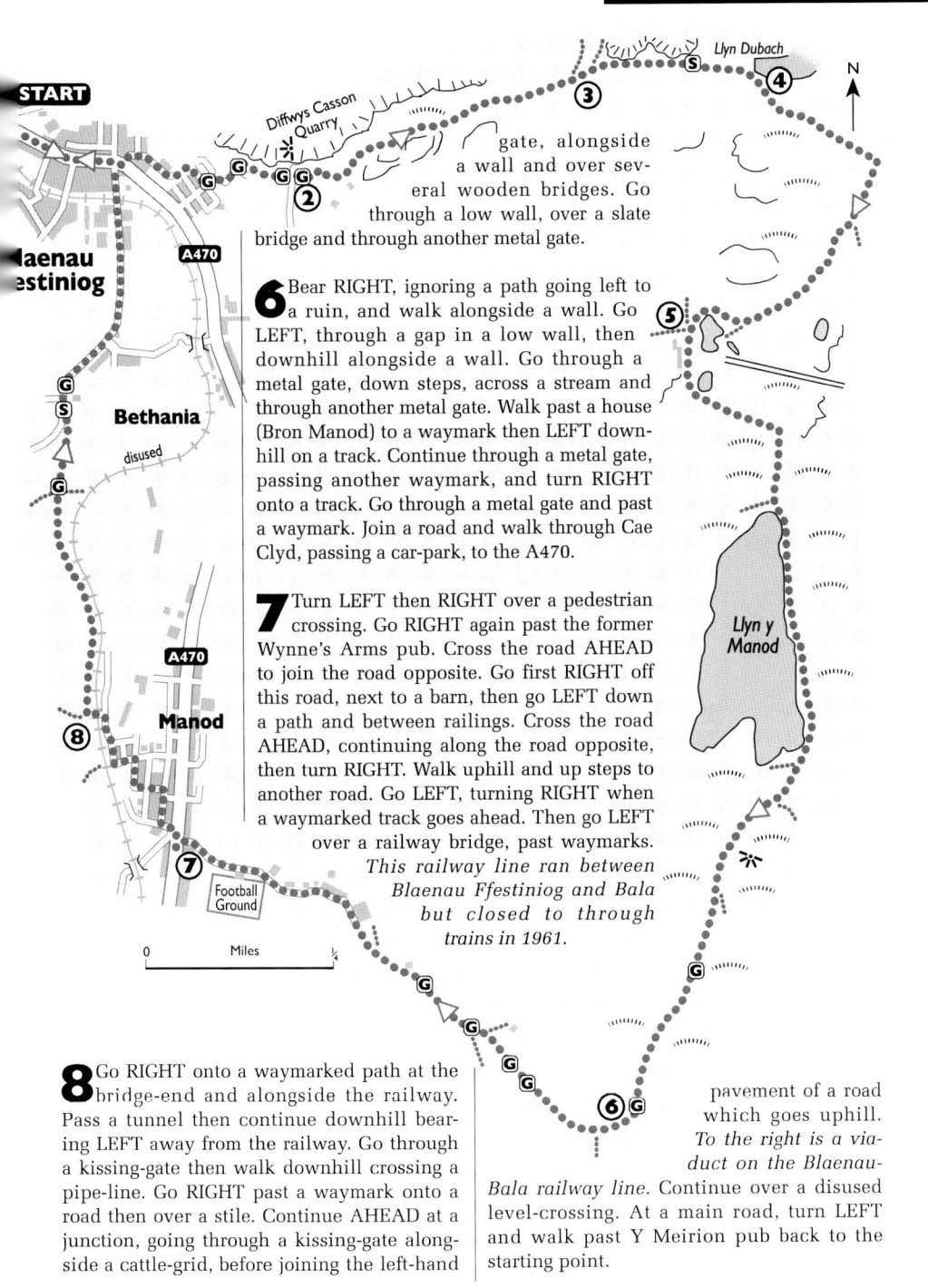

gate, alongside a wall and over several wooden bridges. Go through a low wall, over a slate bridge and through another metal gate.

6 Bear RIGHT, ignoring a path going left to a ruin, and walk alongside a wall. Go LEFT, through a gap in a low wall, then downhill alongside a wall. Go through a metal gate, down steps, across a stream and through another metal gate. Walk past a house (Bron Manod) to a waymark then LEFT downhill on a track. Continue through a metal gate, passing another waymark, and turn RIGHT onto a track. Go through a metal gate and past a waymark. Join a road and walk through Cae Clyd, passing a car-park, to the A470.

7 Turn LEFT then RIGHT over a pedestrian crossing. Go RIGHT again past the former Wynne's Arms pub. Cross the road AHEAD to join the road opposite. Go first RIGHT off this road, next to a barn, then go LEFT down a path and between railings. Cross the road AHEAD, continuing along the road opposite, then turn RIGHT. Walk uphill and up steps to another road. Go LEFT, turning RIGHT when a waymarked track goes ahead. Then go LEFT over a railway bridge, past waymarks. *This railway line ran between Blaenau Ffestiniog and Bala but closed to through trains in 1961.*

8 Go RIGHT onto a waymarked path at the bridge-end and alongside the railway. Pass a tunnel then continue downhill bearing LEFT away from the railway. Go through a kissing-gate then walk downhill crossing a pipe-line. Go RIGHT past a waymark onto a road then over a stile. Continue AHEAD at a junction, going through a kissing-gate alongside a cattle-grid, before joining the left-hand pavement of a road which goes uphill. *To the right is a viaduct on the Blaenau-Bala railway line.* Continue over a disused level-crossing. At a main road, turn LEFT and walk past Y Meirion pub back to the starting point.

WALK 2
BLAENAU FFESTINIOG & THE FFESTINIOG RAILWAY

DESCRIPTION A 3 mile walk which takes you high above Blaenau Ffestiniog and provides spectacular views over the town. The walk goes over, or under, the Ffestiniog Railway on five occasions, thus providing you with the opportunity of seeing one of the steam-hauled trains on this line. Allow 3 hours.

START Sgwar Rawson/Rawson Square (SH702458) adjoining the Blaenau Ffestiniog railway station and bus terminal.

DIRECTIONS Blaenau Ffestiniog can be reached from Dolgellau via the A470, Porthmadog via the A487/A496 and Betws y Coed via the A5/A470. Park in the car-park near the town-centre and Rawson Square.

BUS & TRAIN SERVICES Buses 35 (from Dolgellau), 1B (from Porthmadog), X1 (from Llandudno and Betws y Coed) and 37 (the Clipa Blaenau local bus) serve Blaenau Ffestiniog. All buses stop in Rawson Square. The railway station adjoins Rawson Square. It is served by mainline trains from Llandudno and Betws y Coed, and by Ffestiniog Railway trains from Porthmadog.

1 Walk across Rawson Square towards the main-line station entrance. Just before it, walk up the steps on the RIGHT. Turn RIGHT past the Isallt Guest-House, then LEFT onto the left-hand pavement of Heol yr Eglwys/Church Street. Cross four roads joining Church Street and pass Blaenau Ffestiniog parish church, St David's. *St David's was completed in 1842 and there is a helpful information-board here.* Turn LEFT at the end of the church-yard. Walk AHEAD over a footbridge crossing the main-line and Ffestiniog railways. *The former line comes from Llandudno and the latter from Porthmadog.* Continue on the right-hand pavement of the road AHEAD. Cross several roads and pass the Eurospar supermarket, then Bowydd View (on the left). Ignore a waymark pointing left. *Soon there is a wonderful view to the south, over the Bowydd valley, to the Rhinog mountains.*

2 At the road-end walk between garages, past a waymark and through a kissing-gate. Continue on a grassy path and uphill on some steps. *There is a good view to the left over Blaenau Ffestiniog now. The mountains to the east are Manod Mawr and Manod Bach. The prominent buildings above the valley on the left are those of Ysgol y Moelwyn School (see Walk 3).* The path continues uphill then becomes less clear. At this point turn RIGHT uphill on rough grass between two low hillocks. When the land levels off you'll see a kissing-gate and waymark AHEAD. Make for this, ignoring another gate on the right. *Ahead of you now are the Moelwyn mountains (from left to right) Moelwyn Bach, Moelwyn Mawr and Moel Yr Hydd.* Go through the gate and AHEAD between a metal fence and a wall. *Glance to the left here and you'll see the village of Llan Ffestiniog (see Walks 17-20) in the distance.*

3 Walk downhill past a waymarked gatepost and a ruined settlement. Continue between walls, then between a rocky hillock and a wall. *Now in sight is the electricity generating station at the foot of Moelwyn Bach (see Walk 15).* Soon go to the LEFT of a fence, past a waymark and a tree. Continue to a metal gate and another waymark. Go through and RIGHT uphill past a house (on the right). Go LEFT at a junction and downhill, bearing RIGHT past some ruined buildings. Go through a metal gate, past a waymark to a road. Carefully cross the road (the A496) to a waymark and stile. Once over, bear HALF-LEFT to another waymark and stile across the field. Go LEFT of a collapsed wall and then RIGHT over the stile.

4 Follow a boggy path between bushes towards two slate posts. Bear LEFT and walk alongside a wall (on the left). Pass a corrugated-iron shed and go through a

WALK 2

wooden gate onto a track. Pass the entrance to Afallon house then go RIGHT across the Barlwyd river to a road. Carefully cross the road and follow the waymarked path opposite between terraced cottages. Go RIGHT behind the right-hand terrace and, near a metal gate, walk LEFT through a tunnel below the Ffestiniog Railway. Follow the path between houses, then LEFT, RIGHT and LEFT again (as waymarked). Walk between walls and through a kissing-gate. Continue uphill as the path becomes stony and passes some trees. Follow it alongside a metal fence (on the left), turning RIGHT downhill then LEFT uphill.

5 Turn sharp RIGHT just before reaching a metal gate. Follow a path downhill to the left of a ditch, making for a distant telegraph pole. Pass this and then a waymark painted on a rock before reaching a spectacular viewpoint. *Blaenau Ffestiniog and its vast spoil-heaps lie before you with the summit of Moel Penamnen beyond.* Walk through a metal gate, then downhill towards the Ffestiniog Railway line. Go through a kissing-gate, turn RIGHT and walk over a railway bridge. Continue across the Afon Barlwyd then AHEAD to a road and waymark. Turn LEFT and walk to a factory entrance. Go RIGHT here and join the road opposite (leading to Bryn Goleu). Go LEFT at a junction, uphill, then between houses.

6 Continue downhill, then go LEFT, following a path alongside a metal fence. Walk over the Ffestiniog Railway line using a level crossing. Then cross the road beyond, turn RIGHT onto the pavement and walk uphill. *You are now passing the site of Blaenau's old LNWR railway station (on the left). This was closed in 1982.* Go LEFT onto the bridge over the railway line from Llandudno. Carefully cross the road, go through railings and down steps to a square. *The imposing building in the square is Blaenau's Market Hall, completed in 1864.* Walk alongside the fence on the left then AHEAD to St David's churchyard. Turn LEFT then RIGHT to return to the starting point.

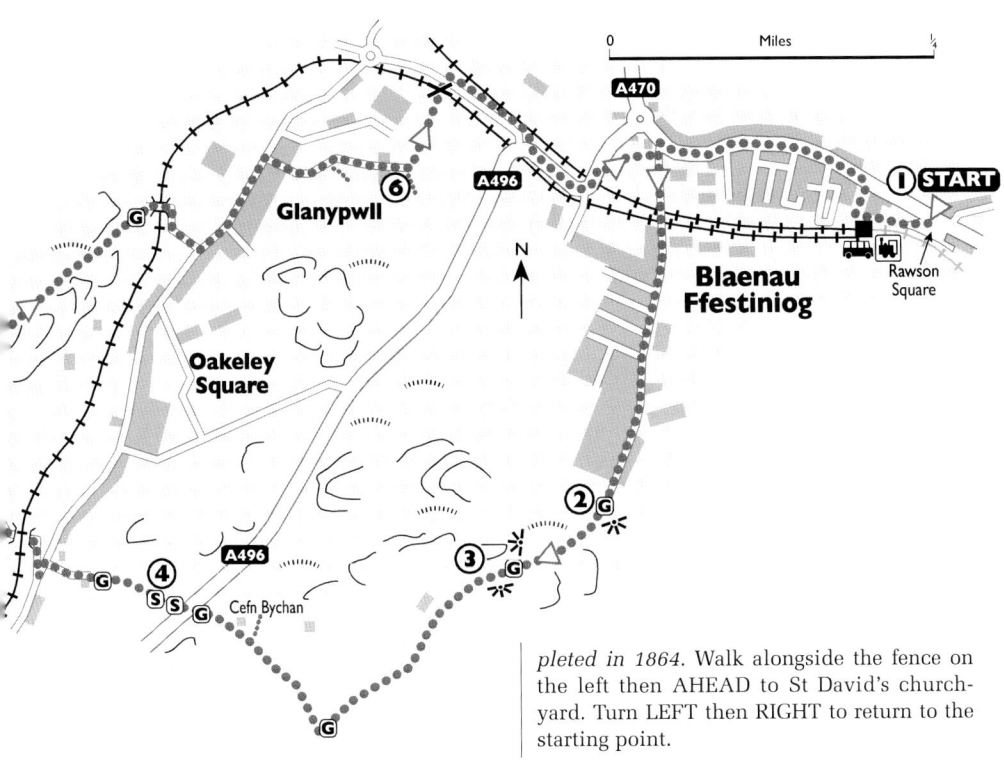

WALK 3
CWM BOWYDD & NEUADD DDU

DESCRIPTION This 2½ mile walk visits one of Blaenau Ffestiniog's most stunning viewpoints, high above the Bowydd Valley. The walk takes you through some wonderful woodlands and past an ancient manor house. Allow 2 hours.
START Sgwar Rawson/Rawson Square (SH702458) adjoining the Blaenau Ffestiniog railway station and bus terminal,.
DIRECTIONS Blaenau Ffestiniog can be reached from Dolgellau via the A470, Porthmadog via the A487/A496 and Betws y Coed via the A5/A470. Park in the car-park near the town-centre and Rawson Square.
BUS AND TRAIN SERVICES Buses 35 (from Dolgellau), 1B (from Porthmadog), X1 (from Llandudno and Betws y Coed) and 37 (the Clipa Blaenau local bus) serve Blaenau Ffestiniog. All buses stop in Rawson Square. The railway station adjoins Rawson Square. It is served by mainline trains from Llandudno and Betws y Coed, and by Ffestiniog Railway trains from Porthmadog.

1 Walk out of Rawson Square past the Ty Gorsaf hotel. Turn RIGHT into Stryd Fawr/High Street, then take the first road RIGHT and cross a bridge over the disused railway line. *This line ran between Blaenau Ffestiniog and Bala but closed to through trains in 1961. The section between Trawsfynydd nuclear power station and Blaenau was reopened in 1982 then closed in 1998.* Ignore a road going left and continue AHEAD. Bear LEFT when the main road turns right. Ignore another road going left and walk past a wall on the left. Continue uphill past a building on the right, then across a car-park past Blaenau Leisure Centre. Join a footpath which goes down steps then RIGHT to a road.

2 Cross the road to join the waymarked road opposite. *The buildings to the right here belong to Ysgol y Moelwyn.* Go through a gate to the RIGHT of a cattle-grid then walk LEFT uphill to a viewpoint and memorial stone surrounded by railings. *The memorial commemorates Dr R D Evans, who helped establish the first hospital in Blaenau Ffestiniog. The view from here south over Cwm Bowydd is superb. This hill-top is called Pen Carreg Defaid (Sheep Crag) and an information-board is helpfully provided. There is a good view of Blaenau Ffestiniog, with its towering spoil-heaps, to the north and east of the hill-top.*

3 Return to the road and go LEFT onto the waymarked path. Walk downhill, through a kissing-gate then down steps to a junction and waymarks. Go LEFT and continue on the path as it winds down through trees. *This is a delightful part of the walk on a well maintained path with views down the Bowydd Valley.* After leaving the trees pass a waymark and then, after a field entrance, walk alongside a fence (on the left) downhill towards a road. Go through a metal gate then LEFT to join the road (ignoring a waymark pointing right). *The buildings you can see to the right below you belong to Cwm Bowydd farm. This settlement dates back to the late 17thC.* Follow the road uphill, crossing the Afon Dubach. Notice the waterfalls on the river as you walk. Go through a gateway and turn RIGHT.

4 Walk over a stile, along a road then bear LEFT at a waymark. Walk uphill through trees with a wall on the left. Pass a pipeline and clearing (on the right). Then walk through a kissing-gate and out of the trees, continuing past a path going left. On a level stretch you'll see a disused railway line on the left. *This is, again, the line between Blaenau and Bala. The mountain above the cemetery you can see across the line is Manod Bach.* Continue alongside the railway, passing a path going left beneath it. Soon walk uphill to a road and waymark alongside a railway bridge. Go RIGHT here then downhill to the gateway to a house. *This is Neuadd Ddu, which dates back to the 17thC and was built in a commanding position above the Bowydd Valley.*

WALK 3

5 Go LEFT alongside a wall then through a metal gate. *Pause here for a good view of the Moelwyn Mountains to the right. The peaks are (from left to right) Moelwyn Bach, Moelwyn Mawr and Moel Yr Hydd.* Ignore a track going left, and follow a path downhill alongside a fence. Then walk uphill, ignoring a field entrance on the left. Go through a metal gate and RIGHT downhill to a track. Go RIGHT onto it then downhill. *Look towards Blaenau Ffestiniog as you walk and you'll see the buildings of Ysgol y Moelwyn high above the end of the valley.*

6 Continue downhill, ignoring a grass track on the right then going through a gateway. The track levels off and goes through a metal gate. Pass a track on the left then the pipeline you saw earlier. Soon pass the waymark and path you followed to Neuadd Ddu. Then return to the road junction at which you turned right earlier. Walk to the RIGHT now through a kissing-gate alongside a cattle-grid. Go LEFT to join the left-hand pavement of a road which takes you uphill (ignore a road going right). *Look to the right where you can see a viaduct on the Blaenau-Bala line.* Continue uphill, passing a road going left and walking over the railway on a level-crossing. At a junction with a main road turn LEFT and walk past Y Meirion pub back to the starting point.

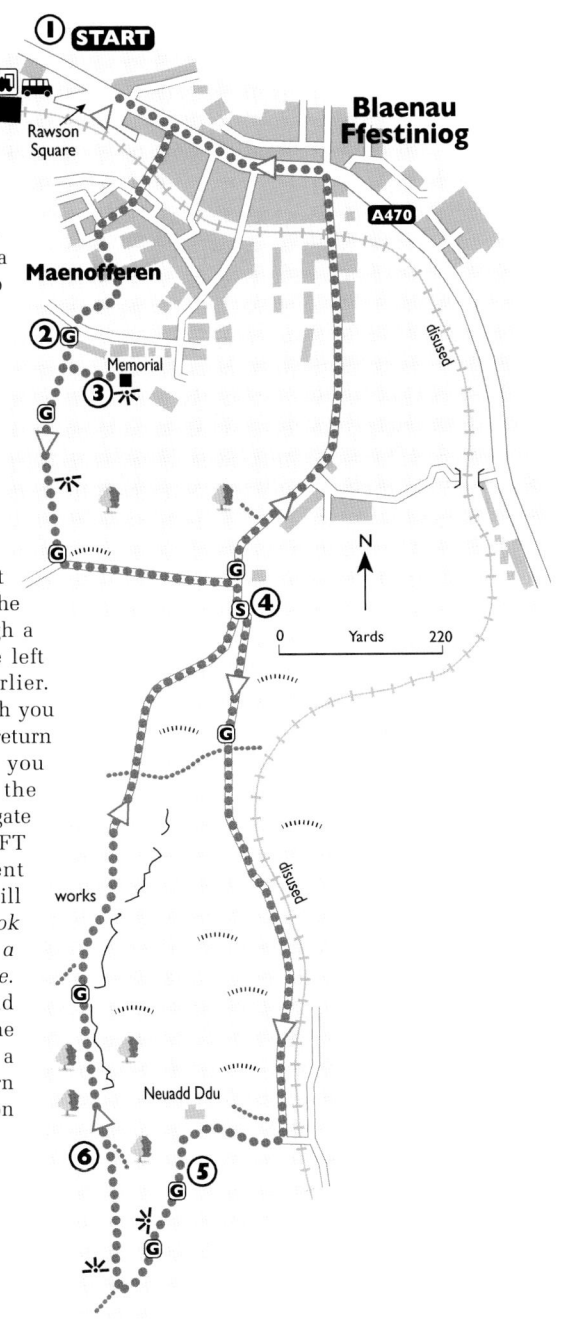

WALK 4
LLYN Y DRUM-BOETH & LLYN BOWYDD

DESCRIPTION A fascinating 4 mile walk which uses tracks and disused inclines to take you past towering spoil-heaps to some wonderful viewpoints, from where Snowdon and many surrounding mountain peaks can be seen. Allow 4 hours.

START Sgwar Rawson/Rawson Square (SH702458) adjoining the Blaenau Ffestiniog railway station and bus terminal.

DIRECTIONS Blaenau Ffestiniog can be reached from Dolgellau via the A470, Porthmadog via the A487/A496 and Betws y Coed via the A5/A470. Park in the car-park near the town-centre and Rawson Square.

BUS & TRAIN SERVICES Buses 35 (from Dolgellau), 1B (from Porthmadog), X1 (from Llandudno and Betws y Coed) and 37 (the Clipa Blaenau local bus between Blaenau and Tanygrisiau) serve Blaenau Ffestiniog. All buses stop in Rawson Square. The railway station adjoins Rawson Square. It is served by mainline trains from Llandudno and Betws y Coed, and by Ffestiniog Railway trains from Porthmadog.

1 Walk out of Rawson Square past the Ty Gorsaf hotel. Turn RIGHT into Stryd Fawr/High Street and walk to Y Meirion pub. Turn LEFT over the nearby pedestrian crossing, then RIGHT past a bus-stop and across Lord Street. Take the next LEFT and walk RIGHT uphill past a waymark. At Brynawel house go LEFT uphill, then RIGHT between houses. At a junction go LEFT past a waymark and through a wooden gate. Walk uphill on a grassy path and through a metal gate. Go HALF-RIGHT, soon crossing a stream. Then bear RIGHT to another metal gate. *Look back here for a view over Blaenau Ffestiniog to the Moelwyn mountains.*

2 Go through the gate and turn LEFT. Go RIGHT through a metal gate onto a track and uphill towards some trees. Turn LEFT up a grassy slope opposite the remains of a stone gate pillar. Walk uphill to a fence and waymark. Go RIGHT, initially alongside the fence, then by a stream. Bear RIGHT then LEFT to join a track going uphill. After a time, and just before the ground levels off, go through a gap in a low wall. Then follow the line of the track to a junction of paths. Go RIGHT at the junction and then LEFT at another junction soon afterwards. Follow the path uphill then up steps. Walk RIGHT near a small building and up an incline to a drum-house (for lowering and hauling up trucks). *A short, optional walk to the RIGHT here takes you along the level top of a spoil-heap to a viewpoint. Note that, on your return to Blaenau, the LEFT turn down steps near the building at the bottom of the incline is easy to miss.*

3 Walk past the drum-house, a waymark and some haulage equipment. Go HALF-LEFT up the grassy hillside, walking to the LEFT of the spoil-heap above you. Then, when the ground levels off, continue AHEAD in the middle of rough ground between workings. Make for the lowest point AHEAD, a gap where a spoil-heap and tramway meet, behind which is a solitary tree on the distance.

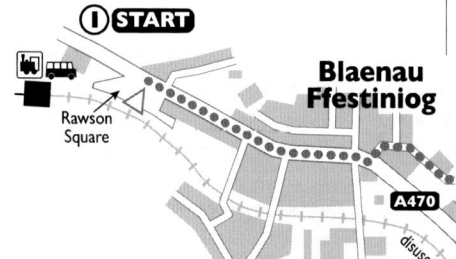

WALK 4

Walk up a slate path past a large boulder to this point. *Note the reservoir below you to the right. In the distance to the right is Llyn y Manod (see Walk 1) between the peaks of Manod Mawr (left) and Manod Bach.* Continue LEFT, then RIGHT, then LEFT again to Llyn y Drum-Boeth.

4 Bear RIGHT just before the lake and follow the path over the lake's out-flow past an old fence. Walk through a gap in the wall AHEAD (ignore another gap on the right), then bear LEFT, making for another solitary tree at the low end of a minor ridge. Go to the RIGHT of the tree towards the higher ground AHEAD then follow the path LEFT, skirting the high ground, to a wall. Go RIGHT uphill. *Note the ruined building over the wall.* Walk past a wooden post to a stile and waymark. Cross the stile and go RIGHT to the summit of the rocky knoll beyond. *Pause to take in the view from here. Northwards, over Llyn Newydd (left) and Llyn Bowydd (both reservoirs), is the summit of Moel Penamnen. Moel Siabod is north-west of Penamnen, and westwards are the Snowdon ridge and the Glyder range.*

reservoir on the right). Bear RIGHT over a grassy ridge, then LEFT onto an embankment. Turn LEFT onto the track along the embankment. *You are on the tramway which linked Blaenau Ffestiniog with quarries in this area. These included Rhiwbach quarry, north of Manod Mawr, where a school was built, and a teacher employed, to provide for the education of the children of the quarry workers. Each Monday the school-teacher travelled from Blaenau along the tramway to Rhiwbach, and each Friday she returned to town in the same way. Some of the tramway's wooden sleepers are still in place.* Soon the track passes the dam alongside Llyn Newydd and crosses another embankment. Turn LEFT at the end of the embankment and walk over rough ground alongside a low ridge on the right. Make for the ruin in the distance AHEAD, first descending to cross a stream near the remains of a quarry. Walk uphill away from the stream, then bear LEFT to a low rocky summit. From here go HALF-RIGHT towards the ruin, then LEFT onto the knoll above the stile. Go RIGHT, cross the stile, then retrace your steps to Blaenau Ffestiniog *(see Stage 2 note).*

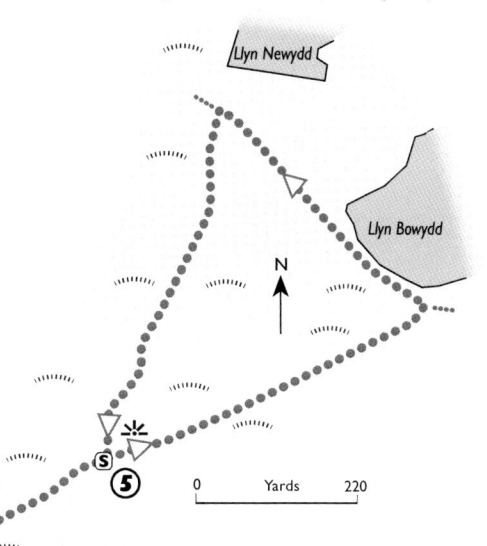

5 ***This stage is optional*** as it constitutes a circular walk past Llyn Bowydd and Llyn Newydd back to the stile. It follows rights-of-way throughout but the paths over rough ground have largely disappeared. Please, therefore, **do not** attempt the route in foggy conditions. Walk away from the stile alongside the wall. Soon bear HALF-LEFT downhill towards the right-hand end of the embankment in front of Llyn Bowydd (the

WALK 5
ST DAVID'S CHURCH & PEN CARREG DEFAID

DESCRIPTION On this 2 mile walk you'll follow a path down into the beautiful valley which lies to the south of the centre of Blaenau Ffestiniog. Indeed, the peaceful countryside will make you feel as if you're miles away from the largest town in Meirionnydd. Allow 2 hours.

START Sgwar Rawson/Rawson Square (SH702458) adjoining the railway station and bus terminal.

DIRECTIONS Blaenau Ffestiniog can be reached from Dolgellau via the A470, Porthmadog via the A487/A496 and Betws y Coed via the A5/A470. Park in the car-park near the town-centre and Rawson Square.

BUS & TRAIN SERVICES Buses 35 (from Dolgellau), 1B (from Porthmadog), X1 (from Llandudno and Betws y Coed) and 37 (the Clipa Blaenau local bus between Blaenau and Tanygrisiau) serve Blaenau Ffestiniog. All buses stop in Rawson Square. The railway station adjoins Rawson Square. It is served by mainline trains from Llandudno and Betws y Coed, and by Ffestiniog Railway trains from Porthmadog.

1 Walk from the information-board in Rawson Square towards the main road. Go up steps and LEFT into Heol yr Eglwys/Church Street. Walk uphill past the Isallt guest-house. Cross four roads joining Church Street and pass Blaenau Ffestiniog parish church, St David's. *St David's was completed in 1842. There is a helpful information-board by the entrance.* Go LEFT at the end of the church-yard then HALF-RIGHT across a square. *The imposing building in the square is Blaenau's Market Hall, completed in 1864.* Join the right-hand pavement of the car-park beyond, continuing alongside a wooden fence, then go up steps to a road.

2 Carefully cross the road, turn LEFT and follow the pavement across a bridge and RIGHT. *The bridge crosses the railway line from Llandudno and Betws-y-Coed.* Pass a bus-stop and go RIGHT when the main road turns left. Follow the pavement downhill. *The station site on the RIGHT is that of Blaenau's old LNWR railway station. This was closed in 1982.* Soon the pavement widens and you arrive at the entrance to an industrial estate. Go LEFT across the road here and through gates over a level-crossing. *The crossing belongs to the Ffestiniog Railway whose line comes from Porthmadog. The trains are usually steam-hauled.*

3 Continue on a footpath past a house, soon walking between a high wire fence and houses. Ignore a path going right between walls and continue on an unmade path which bears LEFT alongside a fence and becomes a track. At a main road turn RIGHT then go LEFT, carefully crossing this road to join the minor road opposite. Take the first road on the RIGHT and follow this uphill, ignoring a cycle trail going right. Continue on this road, following it LEFT. *At this point look RIGHT for a view of the Moelwyn mountains (from left to right) Moelwyn Bach, Moelwyn Mawr and Moel yr Hydd.* Pass Arfryn house and roads going left. Walk on the right-hand pavement until you reach a road at right-angles. Cross the road (Tai Taliesyn) and go LEFT then RIGHT onto a back road. Ignore a path going left then turn LEFT and walk down steps to a road. Turn RIGHT then cross the road to a waymark. *Pause here for a view south over the Bowydd Valley towards Llan Ffestiniog (see Walks 17-20).*

4 Follow a path down steps then downhill past a house (on the left) and through a kissing-gate. Continue downhill then on the level to a junction of paths alongside a waymark post. *(The buildings you can see in the valley belong to Cwm Bowydd farm: see Walk 7).* Turn LEFT here and walk downhill towards a wall (on the right). Follow the path RIGHT over stone slabs and then a metal footbridge across the Afon Bowydd. Bear LEFT then RIGHT and uphill, over a water channel and through a kissing-gate with waymark. Walk to another waymark alongside a wall. Go LEFT here and continue

WALK 5

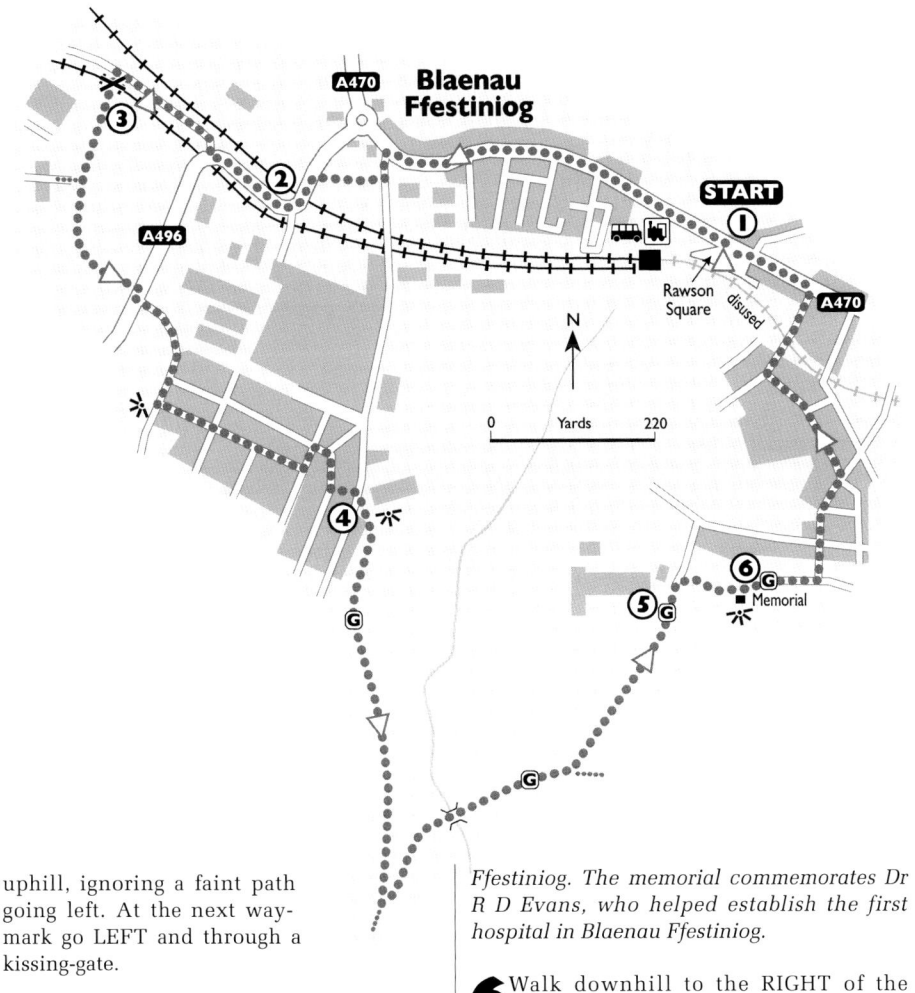

uphill, ignoring a faint path going left. At the next waymark go LEFT and through a kissing-gate.

5 Continue up steps past another waymark then go LEFT uphill towards buildings and a road. *The buildings belong to Ysgol y Moelwyn and were opened in 1901.* Turn RIGHT here and walk uphill to the memorial you can see above you. *The view from here is magnificent, with Cadair Idris and the Rhinog mountains in the distance, the Moelwyn mountains to the right and the Bowydd Valley below. The hilltop is called Pen Carreg Defaid/Sheep Crag and there is a useful information-board. The hilltop also provides a good view of the spoil-heaps, inclines and cliffs which dominate Blaenau Ffestiniog. The memorial commemorates Dr R D Evans, who helped establish the first hospital in Blaenau Ffestiniog.*

6 Walk downhill to the RIGHT of the noticeboard, go through a kissing-gate then between walls down to a road and Blaenau Ffestiniog health-centre. Go LEFT to a junction, cross the road at right-angles, then continue AHEAD on the left-hand pavement of the road opposite. Turn LEFT at the sign 'Canolfan Maenofferen', pass the town library, and walk downhill to a road junction. Turn RIGHT, pass a road on the right, walk over a railway bridge *(this is over the former Blaenau Ffestiniog to Bala line)* and continue to a main road. Turn LEFT, pass the Ty Gorsaf hotel and return to the starting point.

WALK 6
AFON DUBACH & TAN Y BRYN

DESCRIPTION A 3 mile walk which crosses the Afon Dubach then explores the lower reaches of the Bowydd valley. It passes the quiet settlement of Tan y Bryn then returns through woodland to cross the Dubach river once more. Allow 2½ hours.

START Sgwar Rawson/Rawson Square (SH702458) adjoining the railway station and bus terminal.

DIRECTIONS Blaenau Ffestiniog can be reached from Dolgellau via the A470, Porthmadog via the A487/A496 and Betws y Coed via the A5/A470. Park in the car-park near the town-centre and Rawson Square.

BUS & TRAIN SERVICES Buses 35 (from Dolgellau), 1B (from Porthmadog), X1 (from Llandudno and Betws y Coed) and 37 (the Clipa Blaenau local bus between Blaenau and Tanygrisiau) serve Blaenau Ffestiniog. All buses stop in Rawson Square. The railway station adjoins Rawson Square. It is served by mainline trains from Llandudno and Betws y Coed, and by Ffestiniog Railway trains from Porthmadog.

1 Walk out of Rawson Square past the Ty Gorsaf hotel. Turn RIGHT into Stryd Fawr/High Street and walk past Y Meirion pub. Continue to a bus-stop and then turn RIGHT into Ffordd Bowydd. Walk over a level crossing and follow the road downhill on the right-hand pavement. *The disused railway line you have just crossed ran between Blaenau Ffestiniog and Bala but closed to through trains in 1961. The section between Trawsfynydd nuclear power station and Blaenau was reopened in 1982 and closed in 1998. To the left is the viaduct which carried the line.* Continue past a road on the left and a kissing-gate. Then go through a kissing-gate, on the left of a cattle-grid, and walk over the Afon Dubach to a road junction. *The Afon Dubach flows from a lake high in the mountains above Blaenau Ffestiniog (see Walk 1).*

2 Continue AHEAD over a stile, and follow a track which bears RIGHT past waymarks. *The buildings you can see to the right belong to Cwm Bowydd farm (see Walk 7). The settlement dates back to the 17thC. The mountains above you on the right are the Moelwyn range.* Pass trees and then a metal drainage pipe on the left. Then bear LEFT when the track divides. Go through a metal gate and follow the track through a gateway and uphill. Ignore a grassy track going left and continue uphill, passing another track on the left as the ground levels off. Continue through a metal gate and downhill, ignoring a grassy track going left. Soon after bear LEFT when the track divides near a ruined building, cross a stream and bear RIGHT onto a grassy path going downhill. Go through a kissing-gate and alongside a fence, then through a wooden gate. Continue RIGHT past waymarks to a track at right-angles.

3 Go LEFT past a waymark then immediately RIGHT onto grass. Turn RIGHT again, walking alongside a fence and through a metal gate on a grassy track. Go through another metal gate, passing a gate to the house on the right and then a building to the left. *The house is called Tan y Bryn.* Continue AHEAD towards two trees and a gap in a wall. Pass a waymark, cross a stream and walk on the RIGHT of a tumbledown wall. Follow a grassy path, continuing AHEAD towards a stile when the wall goes left. *To the left here you can see the cliffs of Cefn Trwsgl above the Bowydd Valley (see Walk 10).* Cross the stile, continuing on the path which goes RIGHT to a junction with a track. Turn LEFT, cross a stream and walk parallel with the Afon Bowydd on your left. *There is a good view from here of Cwm Bowydd farm AHEAD and, high above the farm, Moelwyn school in Blaenau Ffestiniog.*

4 Pass a concrete and metal drain-cover, then bear RIGHT uphill, skirting trees on the right. Pass a waymark and cross a stile. Go HALF-LEFT and follow waymarks uphill through woodland. When, at the last waymark, the ground levels off, walk HALF-RIGHT to a metal pedestrian gate adjoining a field gate. Continue up a grassy slope to a track. Turn LEFT onto the track and return alongit. Pass the road junction and cattle-

WALK 6

grid, then cross the Afon Dubach. Walk LEFT to join the left-hand pavement of the road beyond, then go LEFT through a kissing-gate.

5 Walk uphill on a path past a wall (on the right) to a track at right-angles. Go RIGHT onto the track and uphill. Go between walls onto a path, then AHEAD under telegraph wires when the path divides. Continue uphill then go LEFT alongside a high wall. Go RIGHT up steps, turn LEFT near a metal gate and walk towards a telegraph pole. Go RIGHT and through another kissing-gate. Continue AHEAD, then turn LEFT. Go RIGHT at Blaenau Ffestiniog health-centre, joining the left-hand pavement of this road. Turn LEFT into Ffordd Wynne, then cross this road and go LEFT to follow the right-hand pavement. Turn RIGHT onto a tarmac footpath near a pedestrian crossing. Follow this uphill, go LEFT at a building, then up steps and across the car-park for Blaenau leisure centre. Bear RIGHT past Caban Bach nursery then continue AHEAD onto the road beyond. Join a road coming in on the left and walk over a railway bridge to the High Street. Turn LEFT and return to the starting point.

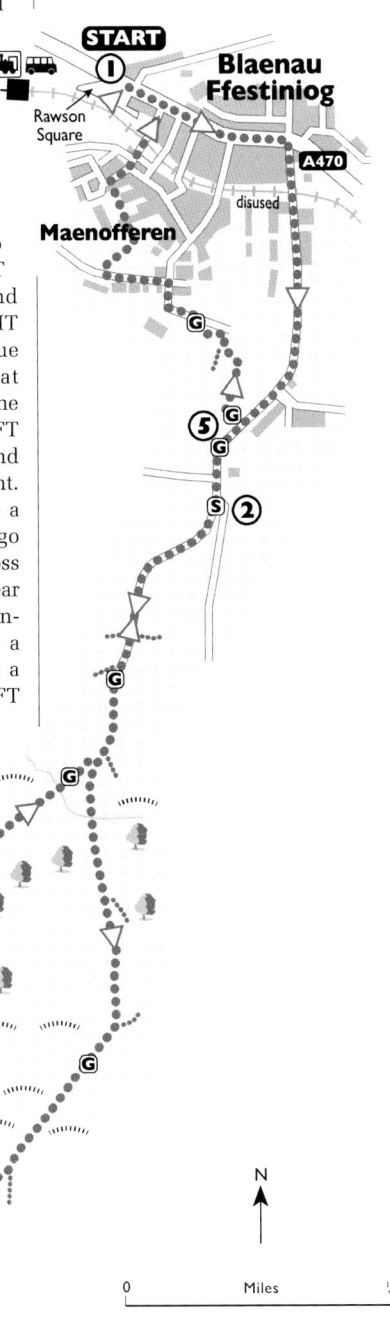

WALK 7
CWM BOWYDD FARM

DESCRIPTION This 2½ mile walk takes you to viewpoints from where there are wonderful views of the Moelwyn mountains and of Cwm Bowydd. On the way you pass Cwm Bowydd farm, an ancient settlement with a Grade 2-listed farmhouse. Allow 2 hours.

START The square (SH702458) adjoining the Blaenau Ffestiniog railway station and bus terminal, recently named Sgwar Rawson/Rawson Square.

DIRECTIONS Blaenau Ffestiniog can be reached from Dolgellau via the A470, Porthmadog via the A487/A496 and Betws y Coed via the A5/A470. Park in the car-park near the town-centre and Rawson Square.

BUS & TRAIN SERVICES Buses 35 (from Dolgellau), 1B (from Porthmadog), X1 (from Llandudno and Betws y Coed) and 37 (the Clipa Blaenau local bus between Blaenau and Tanygrisiau) serve Blaenau Ffestiniog. All buses stop in Rawson Square. The railway station adjoins Rawson Square. It is served by mainline trains from Llandudno and Betws y Coed, and by Ffestiniog Railway trains from Porthmadog.

1 Walk out of Rawson Square past the Ty Gorsaf hotel. Turn RIGHT into Stryd Fawr/High Street and walk to Y Meirion pub. Turn LEFT over the nearby pedestrian crossing, then RIGHT past a bus-stop and across Lord Street. Take the next LEFT and walk RIGHT uphill past a waymark. When the road divides alongside Brynawel house bear RIGHT downhill between houses. Cross a road at right-angles and continue uphill past a waymark onto a path. Go through a wooden gate and up steps. *Pause at the top of the hill for a view over Blaenau to the Moelwyn mountains.* Follow the path down steps, through another wooden gate and past Penycae house. Bear LEFT onto a track, pass a gateway, then go RIGHT onto a waymarked path.

2 Walk downhill, pass another waymark and join a road. Go downhill between houses, ignoring a right turn before turning LEFT onto a path alongside a wooden fence. Follow this RIGHT downhill to a main road. Carefully cross the road and turn LEFT onto the right-hand pavement. Pass a bus-stop and take the first road RIGHT, next to the Don hotel. Walk downhill, ignoring a right-turn, and going LEFT then RIGHT. Turn LEFT under a railway bridge. *This line ran between Blaenau Ffestiniog and Bala but closed to through trains in 1961. The section between Trawsfynydd nuclear power station and Blaenau was reopened in 1982 but finally closed in 1998.* Walk downhill, bearing LEFT past a ruined farm. Continue AHEAD onto a road coming in from the left. Pass two more roads on the left, then cross the road AHEAD. Turn LEFT onto the right-hand pavement of this road and walk past a kissing-gate. Go through the kissing-gate on the left of a cattle-grid to a road-junction.

3 Turn RIGHT and follow the road through a gateway past a waymark. Walk downhill alongside a river (on the right). *This is the Afon Dubach which flows steeply downhill from a lake high above Blaenau (see Walk 1). Look out for the waterfalls as you walk.* Cross the river and continue downhill towards the farm buildings you can see to the left. *This is Cwm Bowydd farm which dates back to the 17thC.* Ignore a metal gate and waymark on the right then follow the road through a gateway and LEFT of a track which continues to the farmhouse. Soon walk through a metal gate and to the LEFT of farm buildings. Continue through two gateways. Pass some barns, go through a gateway and turn RIGHT onto a track alongside a wooden fence. Go LEFT and cross a bridge over the Afon Bowydd. *Like the Dubach river, the Bowydd's source is in the mountains north of Blaenau Ffestiniog (see Walk 4).* Then walk AHEAD, making for the barn across a field.

4 Go to the LEFT of the barn then RIGHT through a metal gate past a waymark. Pass the end of the barn. Then follow a path RIGHT and uphill, on the left of a wall, to a

WALK 7

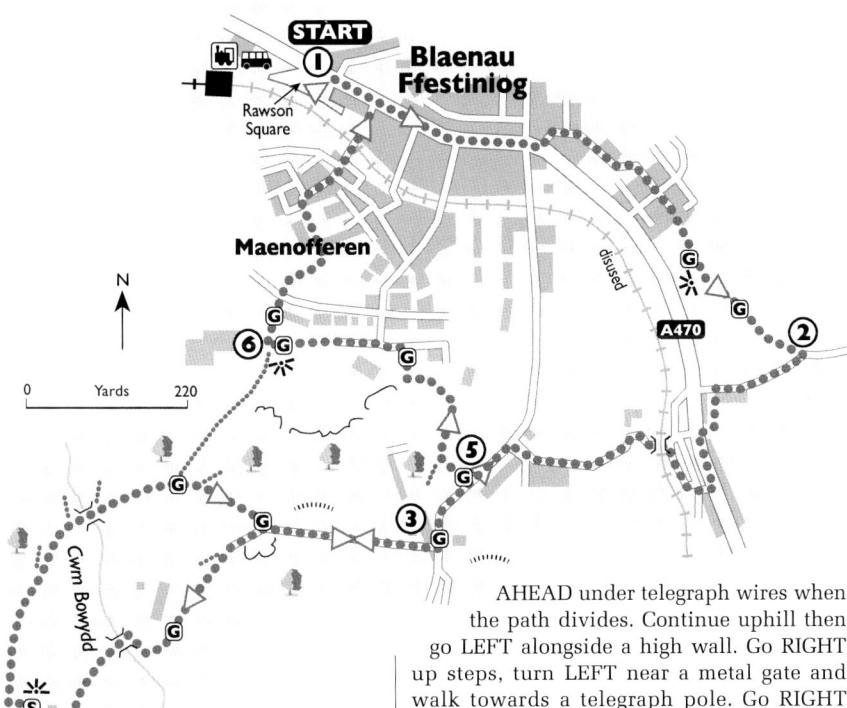

stile. *Pause here for a good view of Ysgol y Moelwyn above you. You'll pass by the school later.* Cross the stile and go RIGHT uphill onto a path. At a waymarked junction bear RIGHT downhill, ignoring a track going left before crossing a metal bridge. Ignore another track on the left and continue AHEAD through a kissing-gate with waymark. At another waymarked junction go AHEAD alongside a wall then RIGHT and downhill. Go through a metal gate and LEFT onto a road. Return over the Afon Dubach, turn LEFT at the road junction and walk through the kissing-gate alongside the cattle-grid. Walk LEFT onto the left-hand pavement of the road beyond, then LEFT through another kissing-gate.

5 Walk uphill past a wall (on the right) to a track at right-angles. Go RIGHT and uphill. Walk between walls onto a path, then AHEAD under telegraph wires when the path divides. Continue uphill then go LEFT alongside a high wall. Go RIGHT up steps, turn LEFT near a metal gate and walk towards a telegraph pole. Go RIGHT and through another kissing-gate. Continue AHEAD, then turn LEFT. Bear LEFT passing Blaenau Ffestiniog health-centre and walk uphill between walls then through a kissing-gate to the memorial and viewpoint of Pen Carreg Defaid (Sheep Crag). *The memorial commemorates Dr R D Evans, who helped establish the first hospital in Blaenau Ffestiniog. From here you can see the Rhinog mountains to the south and the Bowydd valley below. There is a useful information-board.*

6 Walk downhill towards Ysgol y Moelwyn, turn RIGHT, walk through the gate on the left of a cattle-grid and cross the road AHEAD using the pedestrian crossing. Continue uphill on a tarmac footpath, going LEFT at a building, up steps and then across the car-park for Blaenau leisure centre. Bear RIGHT past Caban Bach nursery then continue AHEAD onto the road beyond. Join a road coming in on the left and walk over a railway bridge to the High Street. Turn LEFT and return to the starting point.

17

WALK 8
TY UNCORN & PANT YR YNN MILL

DESCRIPTION This 2 mile walk takes you on a tour of objects and places of interest in central Blaenau Ffestiniog. You then visit a viewpoint, from where there are wonderful views of the Moelwyn mountains, before you walk past Pant yr Ynn Mill, with its dramatic waterfall. The walk is particularly suitable for children. Allow 2 hours.

START Sgwar Rawson/Rawson Square (SH702458) adjoining the Blaenau Ffestiniog railway station and bus terminal.

DIRECTIONS Blaenau Ffestiniog can be reached from Dolgellau via the A470, Porthmadog via the A487/A496 and Betws y Coed via the A5/A470. Park in the car-park near the town-centre and Rawson Square.

BUS & TRAIN SERVICES Buses 35 (from Dolgellau), 1B (from Porthmadog), X1 (from Llandudno and Betws y Coed) and 37 (the Clipa Blaenau local bus) serve Blaenau Ffestiniog. All buses stop in Rawson Square. The railway station adjoins Rawson Square. It is served by mainline trains from Llandudno and Betws y Coed, and by Ffestiniog Railway trains from Porthmadog.

1 Start at the information-board in the centre of Rawson Square. *The square commemorates Blaenau Ffestiniog's links with Patagonia and the information-board describes the development of the local railways.* Walk AHEAD from the square up the steps to the main road. Go LEFT onto the footpath and walk to another information-board. Cross the road using the pedestrian crossing and walk RIGHT. Pass a slate monument and another information-board. You are now in Diffwys Square, named after one of the first quarries. Cross the road AHEAD to the locomotive and trucks which are on display and accessible to children. *The toilets in the nearby car-park began life as a station for the Ffestiniog Railway, whose trains carried slate to Porthmadog.*

2 Pass the station buildings then go LEFT out of the car-park. Cross the road AHEAD, then go RIGHT, walking on the LEFT of the road. *Look LEFT to see Ty Uncorn, one of Blaenau's oldest domestic buildings. It was built to house quarry workers, who lived in four small houses under one roof, with one shared chimney at the centre of the building.* Continue along the road to a T-junction. *Note the immense spoil-heaps here.* Go RIGHT down Lord Street to Stryd Fawr/High Street. Walk RIGHT to another information-board. *The colourful mural on the wall above this is by students from Ysgol y Moelwyn (see Walks 3 and 5).*

3 Cross Lord Street and take the first road LEFT. Follow this RIGHT uphill past a waymark. At Brynawel house bear RIGHT downhill. Cross a road at right-angles and continue uphill past a waymark onto a path. Go through a wooden gate and up steps. *Pause here for a view over the town to the Moelwyn mountains (on the right). The summits are (left to right) Moelwyn Bach, Moelwyn Mawr and Moel yr Hydd.* Go down steps, through another wooden gate and past Penycae house. Bear LEFT onto a track, passing a gateway. Ignore a waymarked path going right and continue on a road. Turn RIGHT at a junction and walk downhill, ignoring a waymark. Pass the entrance to Pant yr Ynn Mill, then look to the left for the waterfall which powered the mill's machinery. *The mill was built in 1845 for the Diffwys quarry. The disused water-wheel can be seen adjoining the end wall of the mill.*

4 Cross a bridge *(over the Afon Dubach: see Walk 6)*, then turn RIGHT and walk down steps, following a path downhill. *Look back for a good view of the mill and waterfall.* Walk RIGHT onto a road and follow it LEFT to a junction. Go RIGHT and pause next to the second of two small terraced houses. *The author John Cowper Powys (1872-1963) lived here for a time. His most famous novel is Owen Glendower.* Walk downhill, then carefully cross the High Street. Turn RIGHT onto the pavement. Pass the Don hotel and go LEFT past a phone box.

WALK 8

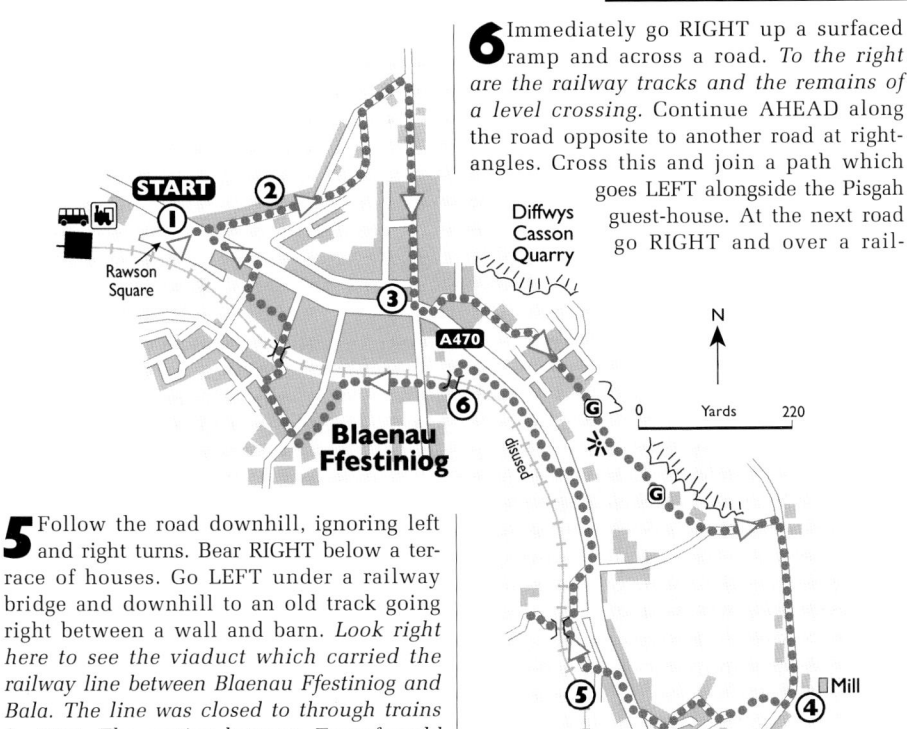

6 Immediately go RIGHT up a surfaced ramp and across a road. *To the right are the railway tracks and the remains of a level crossing.* Continue AHEAD along the road opposite to another road at right-angles. Cross this and join a path which goes LEFT alongside the Pisgah guest-house. At the next road go RIGHT and over a railway bridge. Take the next road LEFT, bear RIGHT past garages then LEFT down steps. Go through railings and RIGHT along the road beyond. Turn LEFT into the High Street and return to the starting point.

5 Follow the road downhill, ignoring left and right turns. Bear RIGHT below a terrace of houses. Go LEFT under a railway bridge and downhill to an old track going right between a wall and barn. *Look right here to see the viaduct which carried the railway line between Blaenau Ffestiniog and Bala. The line was closed to through trains in 1961. The section between Trawsfynydd nuclear power station and Blaenau was reopened in 1982 and finally closed in 1998.* Return under the bridge and turn LEFT uphill. Follow the road past a house. Go LEFT at the High Street, pass a bus-stop then walk LEFT downhill alongside a garage. Go RIGHT behind the garage, ignore a road going right then turn LEFT under another railway bridge.

The Moelwyn mountains

WALK 9
PEN CARREG DEFAID & BRYN EGRYN

DESCRIPTION A 2 mile walk during which you visit a viewpoint overlooking the Bowydd Valley. You then follow a track which takes you past Bryn Egryn house, close to some of Blaenau Ffestiniog's spectacular slate workings. The walk is particularly suitable for children. Allow 2 hours.

START Sgwar Rawson/Rawson Square (SH702458) adjoining the Blaenau Ffestiniog railway station and bus terminal.

DIRECTIONS Blaenau Ffestiniog can be reached from Dolgellau via the A470, Porthmadog via the A487/A496 and Betws y Coed via the A5/A470. Park in the car-park near the town-centre and Rawson Square.

BUS & TRAIN SERVICES Buses 35 (from Dolgellau), 1B (from Porthmadog), X1 (from Llandudno and Betws y Coed) and 37 (the Clipa Blaenau local bus) serve Blaenau Ffestiniog. All buses stop in Rawson Square. The railway station adjoins Rawson Square. It is served by mainline trains from Llandudno and Betws y Coed, and by Ffestiniog Railway trains from Porthmadog.

1 Start at the information-board at the centre of Rawson Square. *The square commemorates Blaenau Ffestiniog's links with Patagonia. Information is provided about these links and about the development of the town's railways.* Walk across the square towards the main-line station entrance. Just before this, walk up the steps on the RIGHT. Turn RIGHT past the Isallt Guest-House, then LEFT onto the left-hand pavement of Heol yr Eglwys/Church Street. Cross four roads joining Church Street and pass Blaenau Ffestiniog parish church, St David's. *St David's was completed in 1842 and there is another helpful information-board here.* Turn LEFT at the end of the church-yard. Walk AHEAD over a footbridge crossing the main-line and Ffestiniog railways. *The former line comes from Llandudno and the latter from Porthmadog.* At the end of the footbridge turn sharp LEFT, then RIGHT into a road alongside the railway lines. Take the first RIGHT then go LEFT into the Square.

2 Turn RIGHT over the road and into the park there. Walk AHEAD then RIGHT through the middle of the park to an exit gateway. *The park contains playgrounds and a bowling green.* Turn LEFT after the gate and cross the road AHEAD. Pass the Eurospar supermarket, cross Bowydd View and continue to a waymark. *Pause here for a view over the Bowydd Valley to the Rhinog mountains to the south.* Return to Bowydd View, turn RIGHT and follow the right-hand pavement back to the Square. Turn RIGHT and pass Bowydd Chapel. Cross the Afon Bowydd and then Baron Road before passing the Blaenau Ffestiniog swimming-pool.

3 Go RIGHT just after Moelwyn school, and through a gate to the RIGHT of a cattle-grid. Re-join the road then walk LEFT uphill to a memorial. *The memorial commemorates Dr R D Evans, who helped establish the first hospital in Blaenau Ffestiniog. The view from this hilltop (Pen Carreg Defaid/Sheep Crag) encompasses the Rhinog mountains ahead in the distance, the Moelwyn mountains to the right and the Bowydd valley below. An information-board is provided.* Return to the road and go LEFT downhill on a waymarked path and through a kissing-gate. Go down steps to a junction and waymarks. Go LEFT, following the path as it winds downhill through trees. After leaving the trees pass a waymark, then, after a field entrance, walk alongside a fence downhill towards a road. Go through a metal gate then LEFT along the road (ignoring a waymark pointing right). *The buildings to the right below you belong to Cwm Bowydd Farm. This settlement dates back to about 1700.*

4 Walk uphill and over the Afon Dubach. *Notice the waterfalls in this fast-flowing river.* Go through a gateway and turn LEFT, walking through a kissing-gate on the RIGHT of a cattle-grid. Cross the river again.

WALK 9

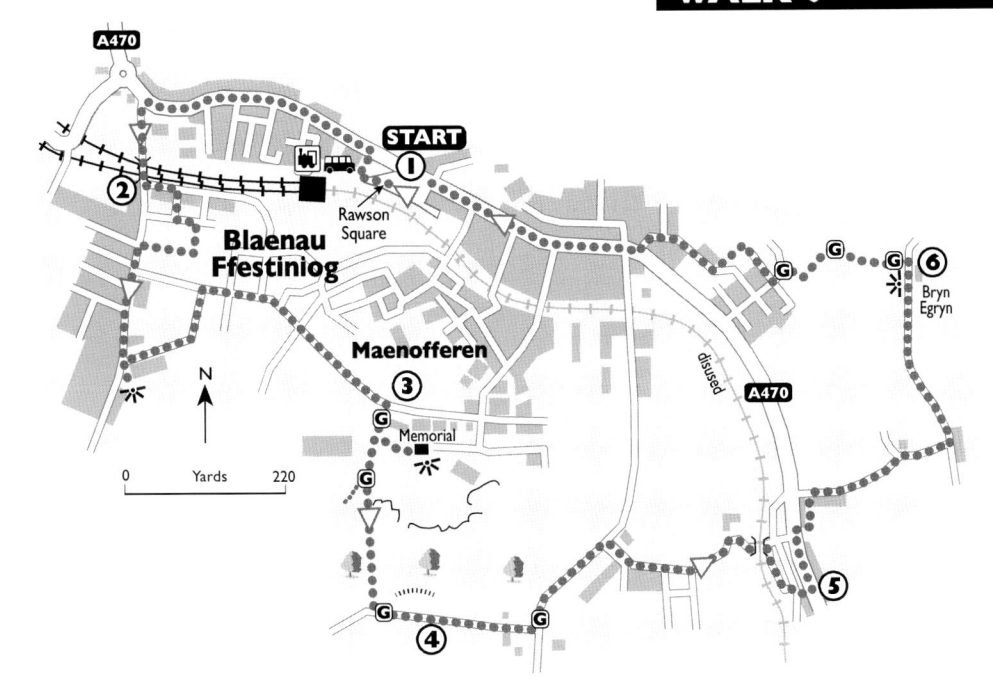

Then join the left-hand footpath and pass two metal gates. Then go RIGHT onto the right-hand footpath of the first road on the right. Walk AHEAD, crossing two roads on the right. Go LEFT at the next junction, passing a limited clearance sign. *Up to the left is the viaduct which carried the railway line between Blaenau Ffestiniog and Bala. The line was closed to through trains in 1961.* Continue uphill, bearing RIGHT past ruined buildings then walking under the railway line. Turn RIGHT and walk uphill past a phone-box to the Don hotel.

5 Walk LEFT along the pavement past a bus-stop to a garage. Carefully cross the road here. Turn LEFT then immediately RIGHT to join a road going right. Follow the footpath then a separate path uphill. At a junction with a road turn RIGHT and walk uphill, ignoring roads to right and left. Then join a waymarked path. Follow this between fences to a waymarked junction and turn RIGHT onto a road. Follow this to a road junction. Walk LEFT here, uphill, passing a gated entrance on the left. Continue on a track past a house to a metal gate on the LEFT. *The house is Bryn Egryn. It was built near paths and tracks used by workers to reach the quarries nearby. Spoil-heaps tower above the house. There is a splendid view from the gate over Blaenau Ffestiniog to the Moelwyn mountain peaks (from left to right) Moelwyn Bach, Moelwyn Mawr and Moel yr Hydd.*

6 Walk through the gate and follow a grassy path downhill. Soon cross a stream on a slate bridge. Walk HALF-LEFT downhill and through another metal gate. Continue downhill, go through a wooden gate and pass a waymark. Turn RIGHT onto a road. Walk between houses, then go LEFT downhill, bearing RIGHT alongside Brynawel house. Continue past a waymark, then go LEFT to a road junction. Turn RIGHT into Stryd Fawr/High Street. Walk across Lord Street then continue AHEAD past a bus-stop. Go LEFT at a pedestrian crossing, then RIGHT past Y Meirion pub and Ty Gorsaf hotel to the starting point.

WALK 10

TAN Y BRYN & CEFN TRWSGL

DESCRIPTION This 3 mile walk takes you on a circular tour of Cwm Bowydd. On the outward journey you cross the Afon Dubach, then walk through woodland to the settlement of Tan y Bryn. On the return you cross the Bowydd river and pass the steep slopes of Cefn Trwsgl. Allow 3 hours.

START Sgwar Rawson/Rawson Square (SH702458) adjoining the Blaenau Ffestiniog railway station and bus terminal.

DIRECTIONS Blaenau Ffestiniog can be reached from Dolgellau via the A470, Porthmadog via the A487/A496 and Betws y Coed via the A5/A470. Park in the car-park near the town-centre and Rawson Square.

BUS & TRAIN SERVICES Buses 35 (from Dolgellau), 1B (from Porthmadog), X1 (from Llandudno and Betws y Coed) and 37 (the Clipa Blaenau local bus between Blaenau and Tanygrisiau) serve Blaenau Ffestiniog. All buses stop in Rawson Square. The railway station adjoins Rawson Square. It is served by mainline trains from Llandudno and Betws y Coed, and by Ffestiniog Railway trains from Porthmadog.

1 Walk out of Rawson Square past the Ty Gorsaf hotel. Turn RIGHT into Stryd Fawr/High Street, then take the first road RIGHT and cross a railway bridge. *This line ran between Blaenau Ffestiniog and Bala but closed to through trains in 1961.* Continue AHEAD when the road goes right and walk past the Caban Bach nursery. Bear LEFT and continue across the Blaenau Ffestiniog leisure centre car-park. Go down steps, RIGHT next to a building, then downhill to a road. Go over the pedestrian crossing and turn LEFT, passing entrances to Ysgol y Moelwyn and a waymark, to join the right-hand pavement of Ffordd Wynne. Go RIGHT at a road junction then turn LEFT past the entrance to Blaenau Ffestiniog Health Centre.

2 Go RIGHT and through a kissing-gate. Continue alongside a wall then bear LEFT, passing a telegraph pole and making for a metal gate. Just before the gate go RIGHT down steps then LEFT alongside a high wall. When the wall goes left walk RIGHT downhill, under telegraph wires to a junction of paths. Bear LEFT, then walk a short distance down a track. Turn LEFT onto a path going downhill towards a wall. Continue downhill and through a kissing-gate. Turn RIGHT, walk through the kissing-gate on the LEFT of a cattle-grid, cross the Afon Dubach and arrive at a road junction. Continue AHEAD over a stile, following a track RIGHT past waymarks. *The buildings to the right below you belong to Cwm Bowydd farm, which dates back to about 1700. The mountains on the right are the Moelwyn range.*

3 Pass a metal pipe, then bear LEFT when the track divides. Go through a metal gate and follow the track through a gateway and uphill, ignoring a grassy track on the left. When the track veers left alongside a gate on the right, walk RIGHT down a grassy slope to a metal pedestrian gate next to a locked field gate. Go through and AHEAD for a short distance. Then walk LEFT to the first of a series of waymarks which guide you downhill through woodland to a stile. Cross this and walk HALF-LEFT downhill past a waymark, skirting trees on the left, to a track. Turn LEFT and walk past a metal drain cover, alongside the Afon Bowydd, to a junction. Turn RIGHT and follow a path to a stile. Cross this and walk uphill then alongside a wall. Continue AHEAD when the wall stops, cross a stream and go through a gap in another wall, making for a shed and caravan. Pass the shed and walk between a fence and tree, ignoring a metal gate into the grounds of a house. *The house is Tan y Bryn.*

4 Walk AHEAD alongside a fence, ignoring a path going right, and then go through a metal gate. Follow a grassy track between fences and AHEAD through a metal gate. Soon, go LEFT then RIGHT onto a track. Follow this through a metal gate or over the adjoining stile, then through a kissing-gate alongside a cattle-grid. Ignore a waymark and gate on the left, and continue to the

22

WALK 10

A496. Turn RIGHT onto the footpath alongside the road, crossing the Bowydd river. Continue along the verge, ignoring field entrances and a road going right. Go RIGHT at a waymark, through a kissing-gate alongside a cattle-grid (ignoring a waymark pointing left) and follow a concrete road downhill then LEFT. Go through two more kissing-gates (the second one waymarked), each alongside a cattle-grid. Then go LEFT up steps and over a way-marked stile. Ignore a path going left and walk alongside a high fence.

5 Walk along a path which takes you uphill towards Blaenau Ffestiniog. *The magnificent cliffs of Cefn Trwsgl are to the left here. At the head of Cwm Bowydd are the buildings of Moelwyn school which you passed earlier.* Soon the path goes up steps, then through a metal gate with waymark. Walk up more steps then AHEAD, ignoring paths going to right and left, and through another metal gate. Ignore a stile on the right and continue to a waymarked junction. Bear LEFT and follow a path uphill. Go through a metal kissing-gate then pass a house and walk up steps to a waymark and road. Bear HALF-LEFT, cross the road then turn RIGHT onto the left-hand pavement.

6 Continue on the pavement, crossing roads going left and passing the Eurospar supermarket. Continue AHEAD over a footbridge crossing the main-line and Ffestiniog railways. *The former line comes from Llandudno and the latter from Porthmadog.* Continue AHEAD alongside a church-yard then turn RIGHT and walk past the entrance to St David's church. Continue on the right-hand pavement of Heol yr Eglwys/Church Street. Cross four roads joining Church Street then turn RIGHT just past the Isallt guesthouse. Go LEFT down steps then return to the starting-point.

WALK 11
BRON MANOD & CAE DU

DESCRIPTION This 1½ mile walk takes you below the Manod mountains to a viewpoint high above the Teigl Valley. From here the Rhinog mountains, to the south, and Cardigan Bay, to the west, can be seen. The walk passes several old settlements and part of the disused Bala to Blaenau Ffestiniog railway line. Allow 1½ hours.

START The car-park in Cae Clyd (SH708443), just off the A470 on the southern outskirts of Blaenau Ffestiniog.

DIRECTIONS Cae Clyd can be reached from Dolgellau via the A470, Porthmadog via the A487/A496/B4391/A470 and Betws y Coed via the A5/A470. From Dolgellau follow the A470 from Llan Ffestiniog to the southern outskirts of Blaenau Ffestiniog. After entering the 30mph speed-limit turn RIGHT just after a pedestrian crossing and drive to Cae Clyd car-park, on the RIGHT. From Porthmadog continue AHEAD onto the B4391 at its junction with the A496 at Pont Talybont. Bear LEFT in Llan Ffestiniog onto the A470 and follow this to the southern outskirts of Blaenau Ffestiniog. After entering the 30mph speed-limit turn RIGHT just after a pedestrian crossing and drive to Cae Clyd car-park, on the RIGHT. From Betws y Coed follow the A470 through Blaenau Ffestiniog for 1½ miles to a junction alongside the former Wynnes Arms pub (on the right). Turn LEFT here and drive to Cae Clyd car-park, on the RIGHT.

BUS & TRAIN SERVICES Buses 35 (from Dolgellau), 1B (from Porthmadog) and X1 (from Llandudno and Betws y Coed) serve Blaenau Ffestiniog. Buses 35 and 1B stop near Cae Clyd. All buses terminate in Rawson Square. The railway station adjoins Rawson Square. It is served by mainline trains from Llandudno and Betws y Coed, and by Ffestiniog Railway trains from Porthmadog.

1 Walk back to the road and go RIGHT along it, ignoring turns to left and right. *The mountain above you to the LEFT is Manod Bach. Soon you'll see (to the RIGHT) the Rhinog mountain ridge, which stretches south from near Trawsfynydd.* Pass a waymark, then walk through a metal gate and follow a track to a junction near a house. Go LEFT through a metal gate as indicated by the waymark, then RIGHT onto a path at another waymark. *You are now passing the house, which is called Bron Manod.* Go through a metal gate, across a slab-bridge and then up steps. Soon go through another metal gate and continue uphill alongside a wall.

2 Walk through a kissing-gate then bear LEFT through a gap in a wall and make for a kissing-gate next to the wall on the left. Go through. *This is a spectacular viewpoint. To the west it's possible to see the village of Llan Ffestiniog (see Walks 17-20) and the length of the Dwyryd valley to the coast. To the right of the Dwyryd is the impressive Moelwyn mountain range with the Stwlan dam conspicuous between Moelwyn Bach (left) and Moelwyn Mawr. Behind you are the dramatic cliffs and screes of Manod Mawr. Below the mountain is Caecanol Mawr, one of the oldest farmhouses in the area (see Walk 19). The valley below the house is the Teigl Valley (see Walks 19 and 20). To the south is Trawsfynydd power station.*

3 Bear RIGHT alongside the wall you've just come through then go LEFT downhill between a waymark and ruined house (Bryn Eithin). Continue on a track, initially between walls. *The village you can see AHEAD, lower down the valley, is Llan Ffestiniog (see Walks 17-20).* Walk downhill then go RIGHT alongside a wall, ignoring a track going left. Walk through two metal gates, ignoring a gate on the left, and follow the track LEFT then downhill and through another metal gate. Walk between barns and a house, then between gateposts onto a road. *The house is called Cae Du.*

4 Walk AHEAD, following the road downhill past two waymarks. Cross a stream (*note the original slate slab-bridge on the right*) and go through a kissing-gate past a waymark on the RIGHT of a cattle-grid. Continue along the road beside a disused railway line. *This line ran between Blaenau*

24

WALK 11

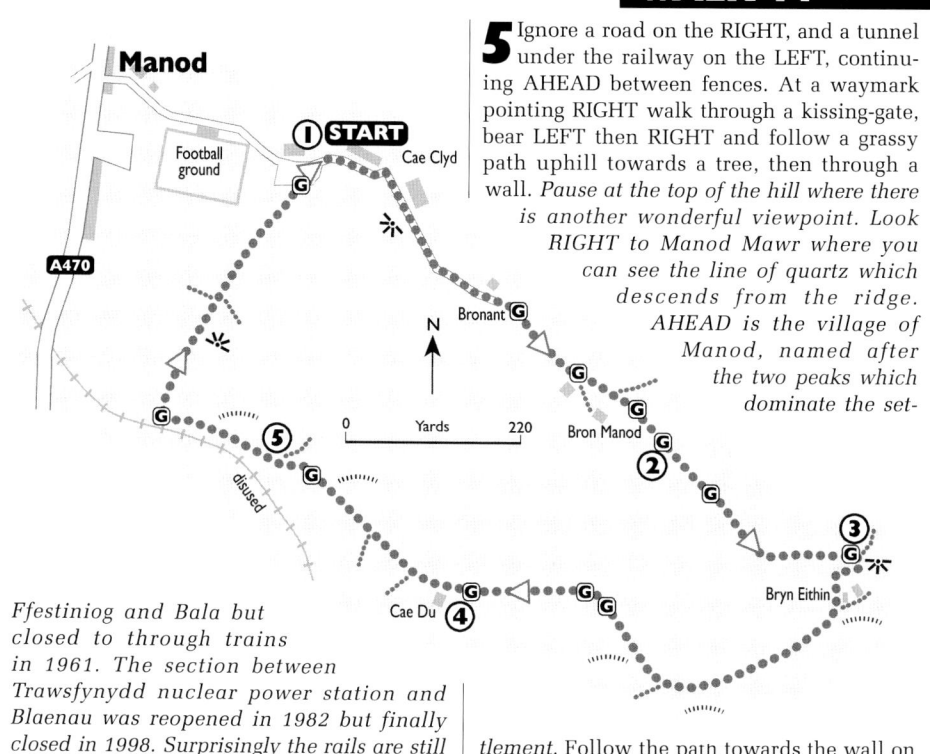

5 Ignore a road on the RIGHT, and a tunnel under the railway on the LEFT, continuing AHEAD between fences. At a waymark pointing RIGHT walk through a kissing-gate, bear LEFT then RIGHT and follow a grassy path uphill towards a tree, then through a wall. *Pause at the top of the hill where there is another wonderful viewpoint. Look RIGHT to Manod Mawr where you can see the line of quartz which descends from the ridge. AHEAD is the village of Manod, named after the two peaks which dominate the set-*

Ffestiniog and Bala but closed to through trains in 1961. The section between Trawsfynydd nuclear power station and Blaenau was reopened in 1982 but finally closed in 1998. Surprisingly the rails are still in place, however, and many of the notices warning engine drivers to 'Whistle' before level crossings, and pedestrians to 'Stop, look and listen' before crossing the railway, have not been removed.

tlement. Follow the path towards the wall on the RIGHT, then LEFT downhill, ignoring a kissing-gate in the wall. Walk through a kissing-gate, over a stream and past a waymark to the starting point.

Manod Mawr

WALK 12
CAE CLYD & NEUADD DDU

DESCRIPTION An interesting 1½ mile walk which provides wonderful views of the Moelwyn mountains. It takes you under the disused Bala to Blaenau Ffestiniog railway line, then past an old farmhouse in a splendid setting above the Bowydd valley. Allow 1½ hours.
START The car-park in Cae Clyd (SH708443), just off the A470 on the southern outskirts of Blaenau Ffestiniog.
DIRECTIONS Cae Clyd can be reached from Dolgellau via the A470, Porthmadog via the A487/A496/B4391/A470 and Betws y Coed via the A5/A470. From Dolgellau follow the A470 from Llan Ffestiniog to the southern outskirts of Blaenau Ffestiniog. After entering the 30mph speed-limit turn RIGHT just after a pedestrian crossing and drive to Cae Clyd car-park, on the RIGHT. From Porthmadog continue AHEAD onto the B4391 at its junction with the A496 at Pont Talybont. Bear LEFT in Llan Ffestiniog onto the A470 and follow this to the southern outskirts of Blaenau Ffestiniog. After entering the 30mph speed-limit turn RIGHT just after a pedestrian crossing and drive to Cae Clyd car-park, on the RIGHT. From Betws y Coed follow the A470 through Blaenau Ffestiniog for 1½ miles to a junction opposite the former Wynnes Arms pub (on the right). Turn LEFT here and drive to Cae Clyd car-park, on the RIGHT.
BUS & TRAIN SERVICES Buses 35 (from Dolgellau), 1B (from Porthmadog) and X1 (from Llandudno and Betws y Coed) serve Blaenau Ffestiniog. Buses 35 and 1B stop near Cae Clyd. All buses terminate in Rawson Square. The railway station adjoins Rawson Square. It is served by mainline trains from Llandudno and Betws y Coed, and by Ffestiniog Railway trains from Porthmadog.

1 Walk away from the road across the car-park to a waymark. Continue past this, across a stream and through a kissing-gate. Follow a grassy path uphill towards a wall and fence on the left. Walk parallel with the wall and under power lines. Then bear RIGHT at a junction of paths, near a kissing-gate in the wall. *There is a good view of the Moelwyn mountains ahead of you here. The peaks are (from left to right) Moelwyn Bach, Moelwyn Mawr (the highest) and Moel yr Hydd. Note the Stwlan dam high on the mountain-side between the Moelwyn peaks (see Walk 15).* Walk AHEAD, parallel with the power lines, joining a path coming in from the left. Continue under power lines, heading towards a group of trees surrounded by a wall. Bear LEFT past these and walk downhill to a kissing-gate and waymark.

2 Go downhill onto a road, following it to a main road (the A470). Carefully cross the A470 and walk along the road opposite past a terrace of houses to a junction of roads and tracks. Walk AHEAD here, taking a path which goes down steps under a waymarked railway bridge. *This railway line ran between Blaenau Ffestiniog and Bala but closed to through trains in 1961. The section between Trawsfynydd nuclear power station and Blaenau was reopened in 1982 but finally closed in 1998.* Continue downhill on a stony path, then down steps again to arrive at a road. Carefully cross this, bearing HALF-RIGHT to a gate and waymark. Cross the stile in the wall to the right of the gate and join a track which bears RIGHT away from the stile. Notice, uphill on the right, the railway bridge over the road you've just crossed.

3 Follow the track LEFT, ignoring a stile, waymark and metal gate on the right. Go through a metal gate and walk RIGHT uphill past a barn to another metal gate. Once through, turn LEFT onto a path which goes uphill alongside a fence, then a wall, skirting rocks and cliffs on the right. Ignore field entrances on the left as the path steepens and bears RIGHT, hugging the higher ground (*Clogwyn y Wylfa*) on your right. Continue AHEAD through a gateway and over level ground. Then walk downhill to a stile. Cross this and follow a path to a junction of tracks. *There is a good view of Blaenau Ffestiniog ahead here. The prominent buildings on the hilltop belong to Ysgol y Moelwyn and below them is the Bowydd valley (see Walks 5, 6, 7 and 10).*

WALK 12

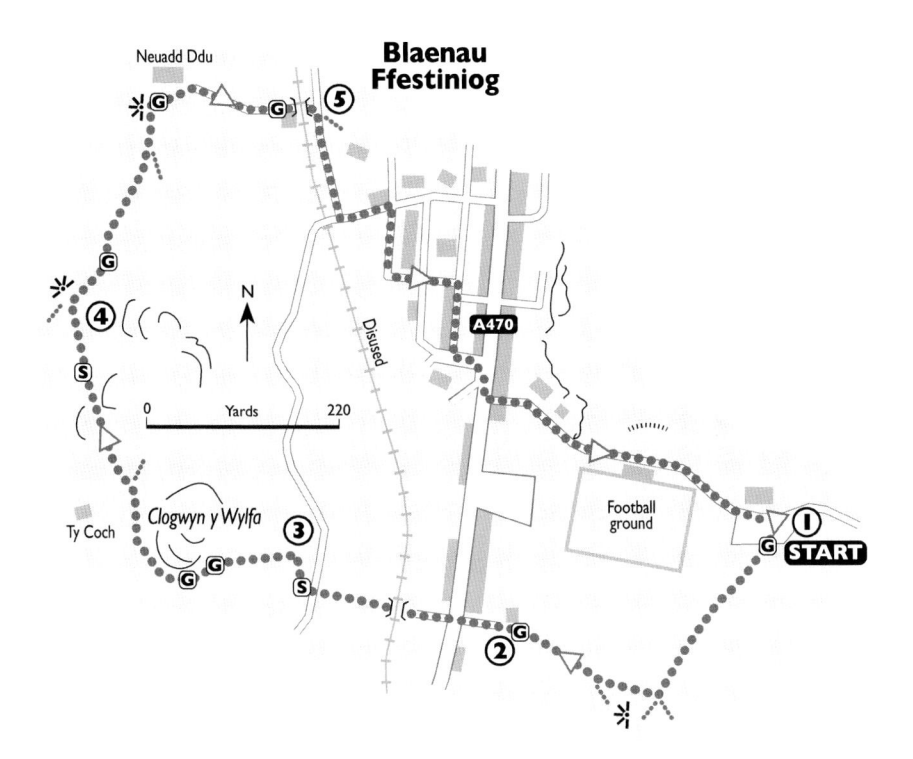

4 Turn RIGHT here and follow the track uphill. Go through a metal gate and AHEAD, initially next to a wall. Ignore field entrances then bear LEFT when a track comes in on the right. Pass a gate on the left and walk through a metal gate. Then go RIGHT onto a road alongside a wooden gate. *This is the entrance to Neuadd Ddu, which dates back to the 17thC. There are views from here over the Bowydd Valley.* Follow the road uphill, passing buildings on the right. Go through a metal gate, passing waymarks and a path going left. Cross a railway bridge.

5 Pass waymarks and turn RIGHT onto the road after the bridge, walking parallel with the railway line. Follow the road LEFT, passing a waymark. Go RIGHT down steps at the end of a fence and walk AHEAD and then LEFT. Cross a road, walk between railings and follow a path between houses. Turn RIGHT and walk to a road junction. Cross the road AHEAD and turn LEFT, walking past the former Wynne's Arms pub. Go RIGHT, following the pavement alongside the A470 past a bus-stop. Carefully walk over the road at the crossing, turn LEFT then RIGHT into Cae Clyd. Walk on the RIGHT of this road and follow it past a football ground to the starting point.

WALK 13
DOLRHEDYN & AFON BARLWYD

DESCRIPTION This 2 mile walk climbs high above Tanygrisiau, passing through tunnels under the Ffestiniog Railway. It provides magnificent views of the Moelwyn mountains and takes you twice over the fast-flowing Barlwyd river. Allow 1½ hours.

START The old post-office (SH 687451) in Tanygrisiau centre. This is on the RIGHT a short distance further into the village from the lay-by mentioned below.

DIRECTIONS Blaenau Ffestiniog can be reached from Dolgellau via the A470, Porthmadog via the A487/A496 and Betws y Coed via the A5/A470. From Dolgellau follow the A470 through Blaenau Ffestiniog to the roundabout to the north of the town. Turn LEFT onto the A496 and follow this for about a mile. Turn RIGHT at a junction marked Ffestiniog Power Station and Tanygrisiau but ignore the immediate left turn for the power station. Continue AHEAD for a short distance and park on the RIGHT in a long lay-by. From Porthmadog turn LEFT at a junction with the A496 marked Ffestiniog Power Station and Tanygrisiau but ignore the immediate left turn for the power station. Continue AHEAD for a short distance and park on the RIGHT in a long lay-by. From Betws-y-Coed turn RIGHT from the A470 onto the A496 at the roundabout on the north of Blaenau Ffestiniog. Follow this for about a mile. Turn RIGHT at a junction marked Ffestiniog Power Station and Tanygrisiau but ignore the immediate left turn for the power station. Continue AHEAD for a short distance and park on the RIGHT in a long lay-by.

BUS & TRAIN SERVICES Buses 35 (from Dolgellau), 1B (from Porthmadog) and X1 (from Llandudno and Betws y Coed) serve Blaenau Ffestiniog. All buses stop in Rawson Square. The railway station adjoins Rawson Square. It is served by mainline trains from Llandudno and Betws y Coed, and by Ffestiniog Railway trains from Porthmadog. Bus 37 (the Clipa Blaenau local bus between Blaenau and Tanygrisiau) runs hourly on Mondays to Saturdays between Rawson Square and Tanygrisiau. There is a bus-stop at the old post-office.

1 With your back to the old post-office cross the road, turn LEFT then go first RIGHT onto Ffordd Dolrhedyn. Walk uphill, under the Ffestiniog Railway line. At a road junction continue uphill, ignoring roads going left and right. Soon you enter the settlement of Dolrhedyn. Turn RIGHT at a waymark onto a path which goes uphill past the end of a terrace of houses. Cross the road and walk uphill to a kissing-gate. Continue on a grassy track. Go through a metal gate onto the tramway from Cwmorthin Quarry (see Walk 16). *To the left is the incline down which trucks carrying slate were lowered on their way to the Ffestiniog Railway at Tanygrisiau. Right is the cutting which was blasted through rock for the tramway.*

2 Walk AHEAD between boulders and through a metal gate with waymark. Follow the path downhill, bearing RIGHT when it divides. Walk under telegraph wires, over rocks to the LEFT of a metal gate and then LEFT alongside a fence. Continue downhill, keeping close to the fence and going RIGHT then LEFT. Cross a stream then follow the path LEFT away from the fence. Walk past trees then between walls and through a kissing-gate. Go RIGHT near a house and waymark. Pass a small garden, then go LEFT and RIGHT onto a tarmac path. Turn LEFT beneath the Ffestiniog Railway. Turn RIGHT after the tunnel and walk behind houses. Then walk LEFT downhill to a road and waymark.

3 Carefully cross the road, pass a waymark and cross a river. *This is the Afon Barlwd which flows from mountains to the north of Blaenau Ffestiniog.* Continue on a track towards Afallon house. Walk LEFT here past a garage and through a gate. Follow a path towards two slate posts then go RIGHT to a slate marker. Here, go HALF-LEFT then RIGHT through bushes, downhill to a stile and waymark. Walk HALF-LEFT across a field to another waymark and over another stile. Carefully cross the A496 road, pass

WALK 13

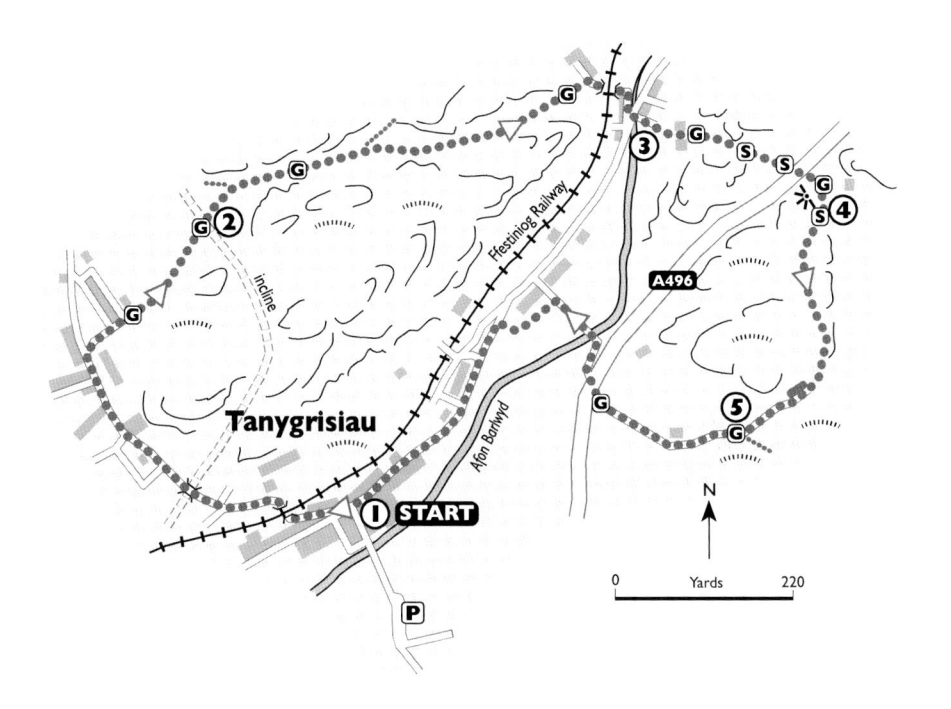

another waymark and walk through a metal gate. Very soon, go RIGHT down steps to a stile and waymark. *There is a good view from here of the Moelwyn mountains to the RIGHT. The summits are (left to right) Moelwyn Bach, Moelwyn Mawr and Moel yr Hydd.*

4 Walk HALF-LEFT parallel with telegraph wires and making for the telegraph pole ahead. Go LEFT here, keeping to the left of a gully between two rocky hillocks ahead. Go RIGHT behind the right-hand hillock and walk downhill towards some trees next to a ruin. Walk over rough ground, then alongside a tumbledown wall to the left of the building. Pass the trees and bear RIGHT to follow an overgrown track downhill alongside a wall to a waymark. *The industrial buildings ahead of you belong to Rehau, a German plastics company which came to Blaenau Ffestiniog in 1978.*

5 Ignore a path going left and continue through a metal gate next to a waymark. Pass a house, Tynddol, ignoring gates on the left, and follow a track going RIGHT to a waymark and metal gate. Go through and carefully cross the A496 again. Go RIGHT onto the pavement, then LEFT onto a minor road. Follow this over the Afon Barlwyd. Turn LEFT into Hafandeg and walk between houses. Follow a tarmac path between concrete posts. Cross the road beyond, passing a waymark. Then cross a main road, turn LEFT, and walk on the RIGHT of the road back to the starting point.

WALK 14
AFON CWMORTHIN

DESCRIPTION A varied 1½ mile walk which takes you past Tanygrisiau Reservoir then to a footbridge over the Afon Cwmorthin from where you can see the dramatic waterfalls on the river. The Cwmorthin flows into the reservoir to the south of which are the Rhinog mountains. Allow 1½ hours.

START The old post-office (SH 687451) in Tanygrisiau centre. This is on the RIGHT a short distance further into the village from the lay-by mentioned below.

DIRECTIONS Blaenau Ffestiniog can be reached from Dolgellau via the A470, Porthmadog via the A487/A496 and Betws y Coed via the A5/A470. From Dolgellau follow the A470 through Blaenau Ffestiniog to the roundabout to the north of the town. Turn LEFT onto the A496 and follow this for about a mile. Turn RIGHT at a junction marked Ffestiniog Power Station and Tanygrisiau but ignore the immediate left turn for the power station. Continue AHEAD for a short distance and park on the RIGHT in a long lay-by. From Porthmadog turn LEFT at a junction with the A496 marked Ffestiniog Power Station and Tanygrisiau but ignore the immediate left turn for the power station. Continue AHEAD for a short distance and park on the RIGHT in a long lay-by. From Betws-y-Coed turn RIGHT from the A470 onto the A496 at the roundabout on the north of Blaenau Ffestiniog. Follow this for about a mile. Turn RIGHT at a junction marked Ffestiniog Power Station and Tanygrisiau but ignore the immediate left turn for the power station. Continue AHEAD for a short distance and park on the RIGHT in a long lay-by.

BUS & TRAIN SERVICES Buses 35 (from Dolgellau), 1B (from Porthmadog) and X1 (from Llandudno and Betws y Coed) serve Blaenau Ffestiniog. All buses stop in Rawson Square. The railway station adjoins Rawson Square. It is served by mainline trains from Llandudno and Betws y Coed, and by Ffestiniog Railway trains from Porthmadog. Bus 37 (the Clipa Blaenau local bus between Blaenau and Tanygrisiau) runs hourly on Mondays to Saturdays between Rawson Square and Tanygrisiau. There is a bus-stop at the old post-office.

1 With your back to the old post-office take the second road on the LEFT. Walk past a children's playground and bus-stop. Ignore a road going left and walk uphill. Continue AHEAD onto a tarmac path and follow this past a house to a gateway and waymark. Go through and turn RIGHT onto the road beyond. Walk, on the right of the road, past Tanygrisiau station. *The station is on the Ffestiniog Railway line between Porthmadog and Blaenau Ffestiniog, and steam-hauled trains stop here regularly during much of the year.*

2 Ignore a track going right and cross the Afon Cwmorthin. *The river flows into Tanygrisiau Reservoir here. Water from the reservoir is pumped uphill, usually overnight, to Llyn Stwlan high in the Moelwyn mountains. The water is then released, flowing steeply downhill so as to power generators at Ffestiniog Power Station. The power station opened in 1963 and was the first major pumped-storage facility in the UK.* Pass the Lakeside Café and cross the adjoining carpark, making for a noticeboard AHEAD. Go to the LEFT of this, then up some steps to a road. Turn RIGHT here and follow the road over the Ffestiniog Railway line then uphill. *When the road levels off walk up a path on the right for a view of waterfalls on the Cwmorthin river and of the reservoir. The mountain ridge in the distance is the Rhinog chain.*

3 Re-join the road and follow it past two parking-spaces and a gate. Bear LEFT at junction and continue on a minor road to a metal gate. Go through a kissing-gate and follow the road uphill, ignoring gates to left and right. *The mountain peak you can see to the left is Moelwyn Bach.* Go RIGHT onto a waymarked path, cross a stream, walk alongside a fence on your right, and continue downhill to a footbridge over the Afon Cwmorthin. *The bridge is just below a series of spectacular waterfalls on the river (see Walk 16 for*

WALK 14

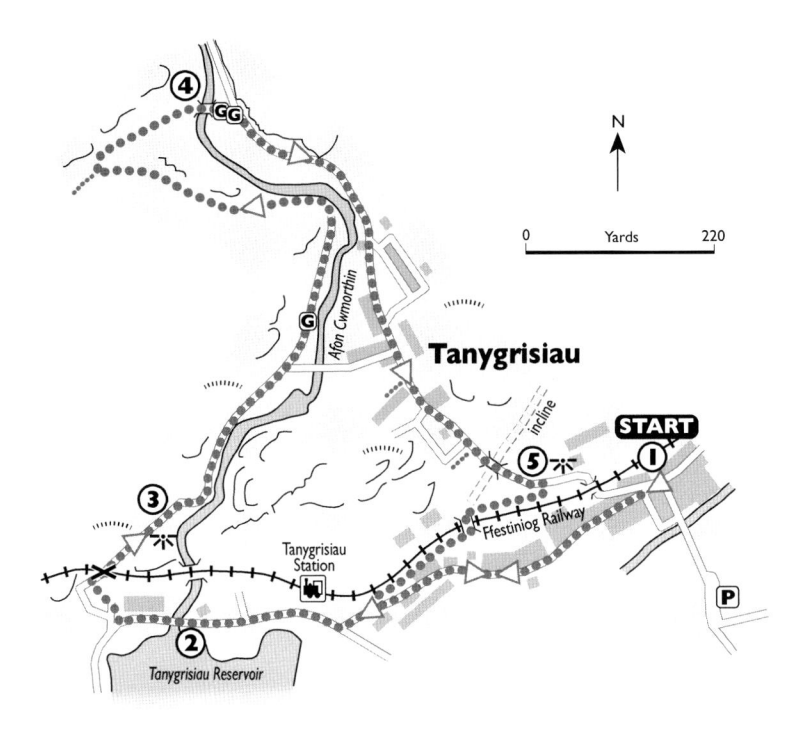

a walk past the falls along the Cwmorthin Valley).

4 Bear RIGHT and follow a path through a kissing-gate into a car-park. Pass waymarks and follow a road downhill alongside the Afon Cwmorthin. Ignore roads going left and right (where there is a bus-shelter) and continue AHEAD downhill, passing a bus-stop and waymark, then a terrace of houses, on the left. Pass a post-box and go over a bridge. *This bridge crosses the tramway which once carried trucks loaded with slate from the quarries in the Cwmorthin Valley down to the Ffestiniog Railway. From Tanygrisiau the slate was taken on the Ffestiniog Railway to Porthmadog from where it was shipped around the world.* Soon you will arrive at a crossroads. *There is a good view over Tanygrisiau and of Moelwyn Bach (to the right) from here.*

5 Turn RIGHT at the crossroads and follow a road downhill to a car-park next to the railway line. Ignoring a wooden gate, bear RIGHT to join a path which goes between walls and passes a house on the right. Walk up steps then go LEFT over a railway bridge and RIGHT down more steps. *This section of the walk is good for views of the Ffestiniog Railway trains.* Continue AHEAD on the path to a parking space and turn LEFT, then LEFT again. From here, retrace your steps to the starting point.

WALK 15
TANYGRISIAU RESERVOIR & MOELWYN QUARRY

DESCRIPTION This 3 mile walk provides wonderful views both of the reservoir and of the Moelwyn mountains above it. The walk also crosses the Ffestiniog Railway on four occasions. Allow 3 hours.

START Lay-by (SH 687449) near the post-office cross-roads in Tanygrisiau centre. Go LEFT from the old post office downhill to the lay-by if arriving by bus.

DIRECTIONS Blaenau Ffestiniog can be reached from Dolgellau via the A470, Porthmadog via the A487/A496 and Betws y Coed via the A5/A470. From Dolgellau follow the A470 through Blaenau Ffestiniog to the roundabout to the north of the town. Turn LEFT onto the A496 and follow this for about a mile. Turn RIGHT at a junction marked Ffestiniog Power Station and Tanygrisiau but ignore the immediate left turn for the power station. Continue AHEAD for a short distance and park on the RIGHT in a long lay-by. From Porthmadog turn LEFT at a junction with the A496 marked Ffestiniog Power Station and Tanygrisiau but ignore the immediate left turn for the power station. Continue AHEAD for a short distance and park on the RIGHT in a long lay-by. From Betws-y-Coed turn RIGHT from the A470 onto the A496 at the roundabout on the north of Blaenau Ffestiniog. Follow this for about a mile. Turn RIGHT at a junction marked Ffestiniog Power Station and Tanygrisiau but ignore the immediate left turn for the power station. Continue AHEAD for a short distance and park on the RIGHT in a long lay-by.

BUS & TRAIN SERVICES Buses 35 (from Dolgellau), 1B (from Porthmadog) and X1 (from Llandudno and Betws y Coed) serve Blaenau Ffestiniog. All buses stop in Rawson Square. Bus 37 (the Clipa Blaenau local bus between Blaenau and Tanygrisiau) runs hourly on Mondays to Saturdays between Rawson Square and Tanygrisiau. There is a bus-stop at the old post-office.

1 Walk away from Tanygrisiau on the left-hand pavement towards the A496 road. Ignore the road to Ffestiniog Power station but turn RIGHT after it and walk along the verge of the A496. Go RIGHT at a waymark and through a kissing-gate. *Pause here for a view of the Moelwyn mountains ahead. To the left is Moelwyn Bach, in the centre is Moelwyn Mawr and, to the right, Moel yr Hydd.* Cross a gated footbridge over the Afon Barlwyd and continue AHEAD uphill over rough ground, making for a waymark. Walk under telegraph wires, then bear HALF-RIGHT, following a path on the left of higher ground and past another waymark. Bear RIGHT again, then LEFT, on what is now a track, to a hilltop and waymark. *There is a good view to the right here, of the Ffestiniog Power Station and the Stwlan Dam, water from which powers the turbines below. Look behind and you can see Blaenau Ffestiniog, with the pointed summit of Moel Penamnen to the north of the town*

2 Walk HALF-RIGHT off the track, passing the waymark and following a path downhill. Go over a stile, then down steps and walk steeply downhill to a junction of paths. Go LEFT here and follow a waymarked path which soon goes uphill then under power-lines before coming to a viewpoint. *Ahead now you can see the northern end of the Rhinog mountain ridge. The mountain above you on the LEFT here is Moel Ystradau. You can see the quarry workings on its lower slopes.* Turn LEFT at a waymark here, ignoring a track which goes right downhill from the viewpoint, and follow a path towards a fence. Bear RIGHT at the fence and walk alongside it to where it ends. Here, ignore a path going left, and walk downhill. Continue over rough ground then go uphill. *There's a good view of the end of the reservoir here.* Look for a waymark AHEAD and make for it. Cross a track here and walk over a bridge, then over two stiles (to be replaced by gates during the summer of 2017) and the Ffestiniog Railway line.

WALK 15

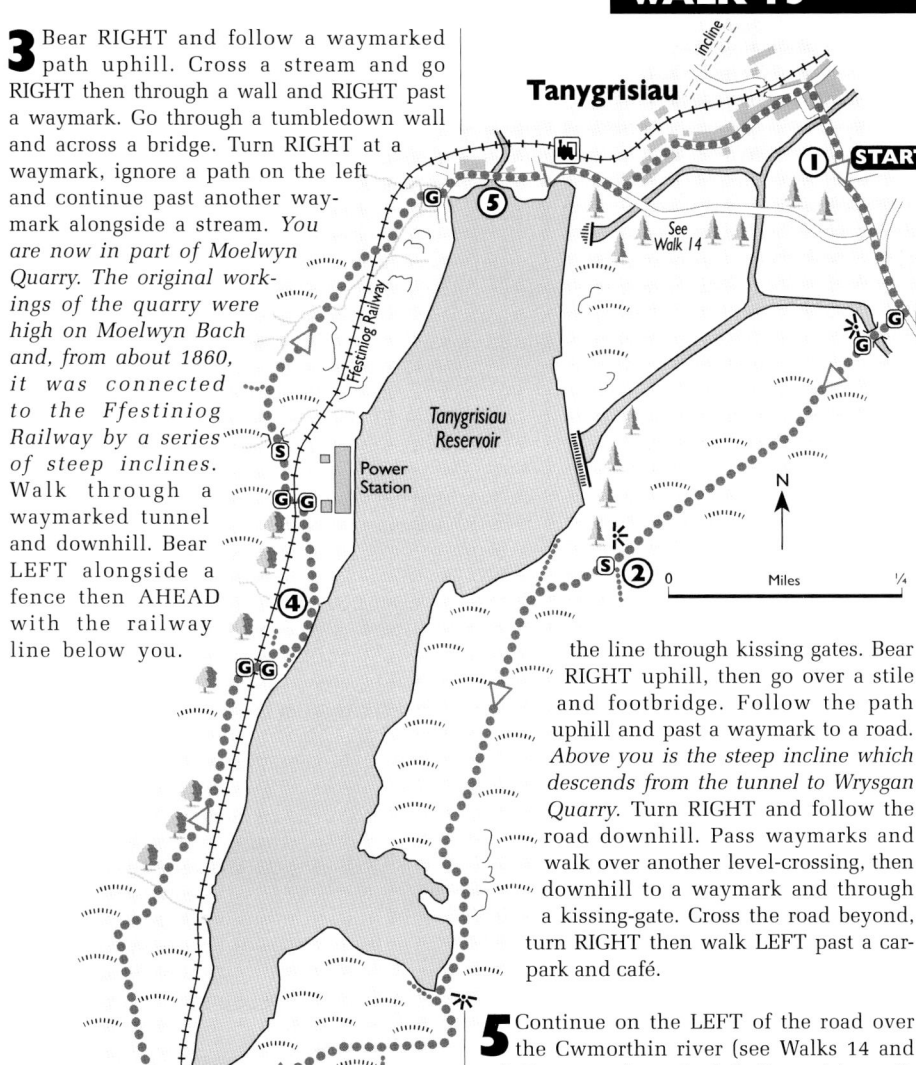

3 Bear RIGHT and follow a waymarked path uphill. Cross a stream and go RIGHT then through a wall and RIGHT past a waymark. Go through a tumbledown wall and across a bridge. Turn RIGHT at a waymark, ignore a path on the left and continue past another waymark alongside a stream. *You are now in part of Moelwyn Quarry. The original workings of the quarry were high on Moelwyn Bach and, from about 1860, it was connected to the Ffestiniog Railway by a series of steep inclines.* Walk through a waymarked tunnel and downhill. Bear LEFT alongside a fence then AHEAD with the railway line below you.

Go RIGHT through a metal gate, across the railway and through another metal gate with waymark. Follow the path LEFT then RIGHT downhill. Ignore a path going left then turn LEFT onto a track passing a waymark.

4 Walk over a stream then bear LEFT at a waymark. Follow a path uphill past another waymark. Walk alongside the Ffestiniog Railway line then go LEFT across the line through kissing gates. Bear RIGHT uphill, then go over a stile and footbridge. Follow the path uphill and past a waymark to a road. *Above you is the steep incline which descends from the tunnel to Wrysgan Quarry.* Turn RIGHT and follow the road downhill. Pass waymarks and walk over another level-crossing, then downhill to a waymark and through a kissing-gate. Cross the road beyond, turn RIGHT then walk LEFT past a car-park and café.

5 Continue on the LEFT of the road over the Cwmorthin river (see Walks 14 and 16). Pass a track on the left, Tanygrisiau railway station and the entrance to the reservoir dam. Then walk LEFT at a waymark, through railings and along a road past a house. Pass a parking area and bear RIGHT, following the road downhill. Pass (on the right) a road and a bus-stop, then join a footpath on the right of the road. Pass a playing area and park, then cross the road and join the left-hand pavement. Pass Tanygrisiau School and at the crossroads beyond either return to the bus-stop or turn RIGHT to return to the lay-by.

WALK 16
THE CWMORTHIN VALLEY

DESCRIPTION A dramatic 3 mile walk during which you climb from Tanygrisiau past magnificent waterfalls into a spectacular valley which once was a centre of slate quarrying. You follow an old tramway past Llyn Cwmorthin to a ruined chapel and the remains of a mining settlement. Allow 3 hours.

START The old post-office (SH 687451) in Tanygrisiau centre. This is on the RIGHT a short distance further into the village from the lay-by mentioned below.

DIRECTIONS Blaenau Ffestiniog can be reached from Dolgellau via the A470, Porthmadog via the A487/A496 and Betws y Coed via the A5/A470. From Dolgellau follow the A470 through Blaenau Ffestiniog to the roundabout to the north of the town. Turn LEFT onto the A496 and follow this for about a mile. Turn RIGHT at a junction marked Ffestiniog Power Station and Tanygrisiau but ignore the immediate left turn for the power station. Continue AHEAD for a short distance and park on the RIGHT in a long lay-by. From Porthmadog turn LEFT at a junction with the A496 marked Ffestiniog Power Station and Tanygrisiau but ignore the immediate left turn for the power station. Continue AHEAD for a short distance and park on the RIGHT in a long lay-by. From Betws-y-Coed turn RIGHT from the A470 onto the A496 at the roundabout on the north of Blaenau Ffestiniog. Follow this for about a mile. Turn RIGHT at a junction marked Ffestiniog Power Station and Tanygrisiau but ignore the immediate left turn for the power station. Continue AHEAD for a short distance and park on the RIGHT in a long lay-by.

BUS & TRAIN SERVICES Buses 35 (from Dolgellau), 1B (from Porthmadog) and X1 (from Llandudno and Betws y Coed) serve Blaenau Ffestiniog. All buses stop in Rawson Square. The railway station adjoins Rawson Square. It is served by mainline trains from Llandudno and Betws y Coed, and by Ffestiniog Railway trains from Porthmadog. Bus 37 (the Clipa Blaenau local bus between Blaenau and Tanygrisiau) runs hourly on Mondays to Saturdays between Rawson Square and Tanygrisiau. There is a bus-stop at the old post-office.

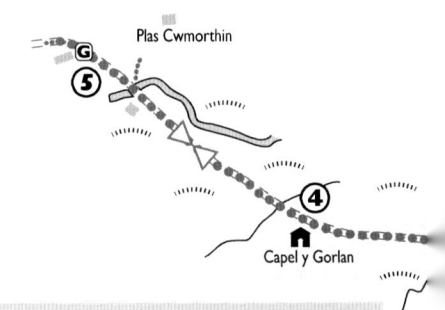

1 With your back to the old post-office take the second road on the LEFT. Walk past a children's playground and bus-stop. Ignore a road going left and walk uphill to a parking space. Turn RIGHT, then RIGHT again onto a path behind houses. Go up steps then LEFT over a railway bridge. *This section of the walk is good for views of the Ffestiniog Railway steam-hauled trains. The railway was opened in 1836 to carry slate from the quarries around Blaenau Ffestiniog to Porthmadog.* Go RIGHT down steps along a path past houses to a car-park.

2 Continue uphill on a road to a junction. *Look RIGHT here for a good view over Tanygrisiau.* Go LEFT over a bridge. *This bridge crosses the remains of the tramway which carried trucks loaded with slate from the quarries in the Cwmorthin Valley down to the Ffestiniog Railway.* Walk uphill, passing a post-box. Ignore a waymark next to a bus-stop then, at a road junction, bear RIGHT. Walk uphill to a car-park, then AHEAD, past waymarks, through a kissing-gate.

3 Continue uphill on a track alongside the Afon Cwmorthin. *The waterfalls on this river are some of the most spectacular in the area.* When the track levels off ignore a track going right and a waymark point-

34

WALK 16

ing left. Bear LEFT at the next junction and continue uphill. *Ahead, across the river, you can see the ruins of Cwmorthin Terrace, houses built by the owners of Cwmorthin Quarry during the 1860s and 1870s.* At the next junction turn LEFT over the river. Walk below Cwmorthin Terrace and through a kissing-gate, following the track as it skirts Llyn Cwmorthin. *On the opposite side of the lake are the remains of Cwmorthin House, built during the 1840s for the quarry manager.* Go through another kissing-gate and continue alongside a slate fence. *You are now following the tramway which was constructed along the valley to connect with the Ffestiniog Railway at Tanygrisiau.* Cross a stream before arriving at Capel y Gorlan. *This impressive chapel was built in 1867 and could hold a congregation of 100. The slate roof was removed during the 1970s.*

4 Continue on the track past a ruin and across a river to the quarry workings at the head of the valley. *To the right is the ruined Plas Cwmorthin, built in 1860 for the manager of Rhosydd Quarry. This quarry is high above the valley along the track you can see ahead. Many of the workers there lived, during the week, in barracks at the remote site.* Walk through a kissing-gate to Conglog Quarry. *The stone pillars you can see are launder pillars which supported troughs supplying water to this small quarry. The now derelict terrace of cottages was built by Rhosydd Quarry in 1865.*

5 Return past Capel y Gorlan and Cwmorthin Terrace, then downhill to the kissing-gate at the start of the track. Turn RIGHT, go through another kissing-gate and across a footbridge over the Cwmorthin river. Walk LEFT at the bridge-end then uphill alongside a fence and across a stream to a road and waymark. Go LEFT here, downhill, ignoring gates left and right. *The mountain peak you can see to the right is Moelwyn Bach.* Walk through a kissing-gate then LEFT at a road junction. Continue to another junction. Turn RIGHT here and retrace your steps over the tramway bridge to the junction you visited earlier. Continue AHEAD, following the road downhill under a railway bridge to the starting point.

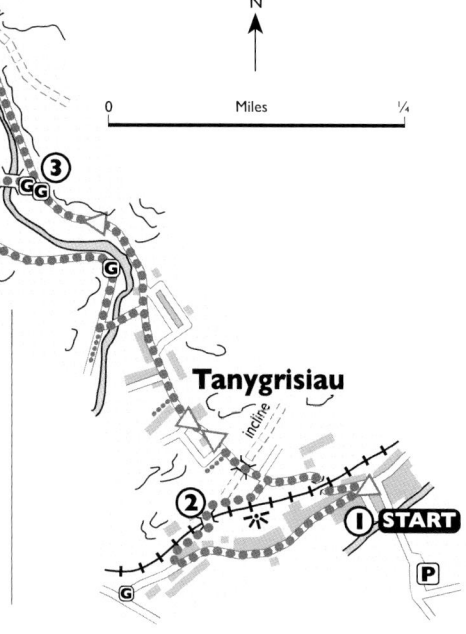

WALK 17
THE CYNFAL WATERFALLS & VALLEY

DESCRIPTION There are spectacular views of the Moelwyn Mountains during this 2½ mile walk. You also visit some magnificent waterfalls and cross two bridges over the Afon Cynfal. Allow 3 hours.

START Y Pengwern community pub in Llan Ffestiniog square (SH700419).

DIRECTIONS Llan Ffestiniog can be reached from Dolgellau via the A470, Porthmadog via the A487/A496/B4391 and Betws y Coed via the A5/A470. Park in the square in the centre of the village adjoining Y Pengwern pub.

BUS & TRAIN SERVICES Buses 35 (from Blaenau Ffestiniog and Dolgellau) and 1B (from Blaenau Ffestiniog and Porthmadog) stop at the Pengwern pub in Llan Ffestiniog. Bus X1 (from Llandudno and Betws y Coed) serves Blaenau Ffestiniog. The town is also served by mainline trains from Llandudno and Betws y Coed, and by Ffestiniog Railway trains from Porthmadog.

1 With your back to the Pengwern pub walk across the square, then over the road to Meirion House. *This Grade II* listed building is one of several in the square which provide evidence of Llan Ffestiniog's past importance as a commercial centre. It's name derives from the county of Meirionnydd and the oldest part of the house is thought to date back to 1411. It was once a bank, as you can see from the sign.* Turn RIGHT and follow the pavement downhill, ignoring a track going left, to a metal gate and waymark. Turn LEFT through the gate and follow a grassy path downhill. *There is a good view from here over the Cynfal valley to the Rhinog mountains. You can also see the Trawsfynydd nuclear power station, built during the 1950s to a design by Basil Spence but now being decommissioned.*

2 Cross a track alongside a gate and waymark, walk down some steps and go through a metal gate. Pass another gate and waymark on the left and continue downhill alongside a fence. Go LEFT through a metal gate, as waymarked, pass a ruined barn and continue AHEAD, keeping to the LEFT of a telegraph pole. Continue downhill to another metal gate and waymark. Go through, cross a stream and walk uphill. Go through another metal gate, then up steps and through a wooden gate. Bear RIGHT and walk to a metal gate with waymark. *Once through look RIGHT for a view of Llan Ffestiniog village and church. Beyond the village is the Moelwyn mountain range, with the Stwlan dam visible below the ridge.*

3 Continue AHEAD alongside a fence, following the track downhill and through a metal gate. Ignore a path going left, cross a stream and walk through a wooden gate into woodland and an information-board about the Cynfal nature reserve. Turn RIGHT onto a path just after the information-board and follow this downhill, then down steps, to a viewpoint above the Cynfal gorge. *The viewpoint is safely enclosed in metal fencing and provides dramatic views of the gorge and waterfalls.* Return to the upper path, turn RIGHT and follow the path above the gorge. Soon look RIGHT for a view of a precipitous rock pillar in the river known as Huw Llwyd's pulpit. *During the 17thC, Llwyd was thought to be a magician. Believing he was safe from evil because the devil was afraid of water, he stood on the rock to preach sermons and converse with spirits.* Ignore minor paths going right, pass another information-board then walk down steps. Cross a footbridge over the Afon Cynfal, going through a metal gate and up steps. Then go RIGHT at waymarks and through a wooden gate.

4 Follow a grassy path through a wooden gate, cross a slate bridge over a stream and go through another wooden gate. *Soon there is another magnificent view of the Moelwyn mountains.* Pass a waymark, cross another stream and go through two more wooden gates. Walk over a third stream and, at a waymark pointing ahead, turn RIGHT and walk downhill. Go down steps and cross another bridge over the Cynfal,

WALK 17

metal gate (on the right) through which you walked earlier. From here return to Llan Ffestiniog square following the route you used initially.

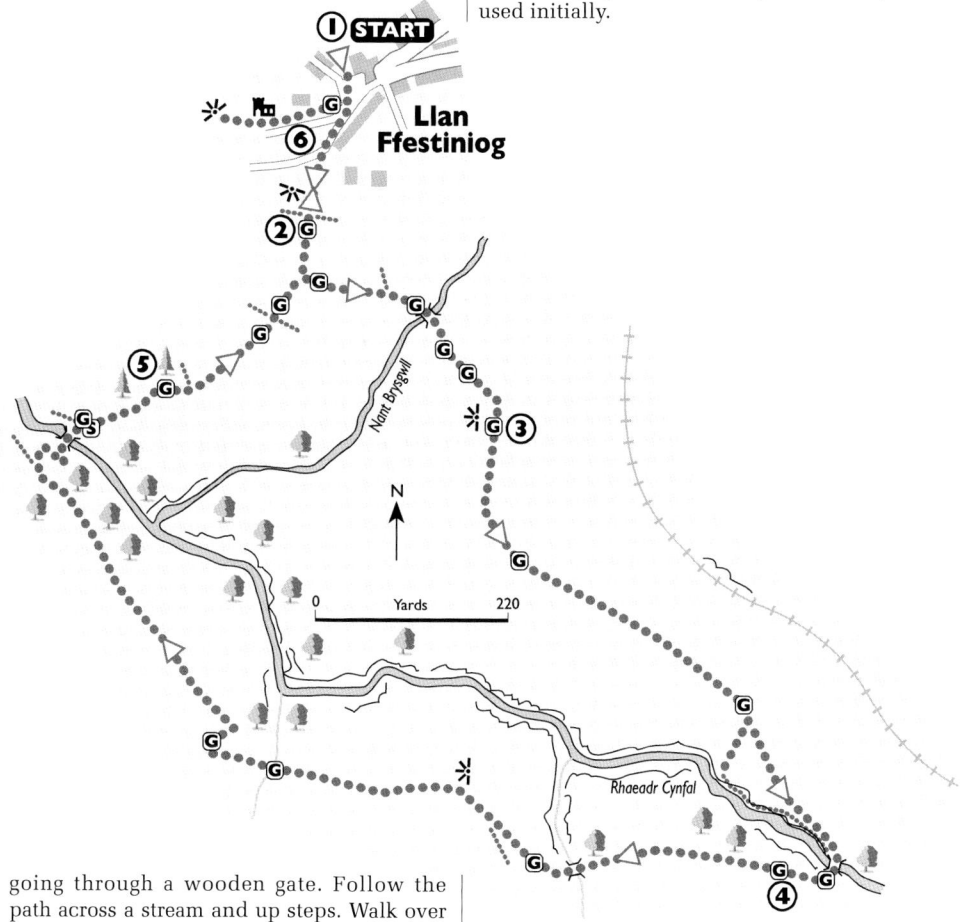

going through a wooden gate. Follow the path across a stream and up steps. Walk over another stream and cross a stile. Follow the path uphill through woodland, up steps and through a metal gate.

5 Turn RIGHT onto a path at right-angles, passing a gate on the right and emerging from the trees. When the path divides bear LEFT and continue uphill across a grassy slope. Then bear LEFT towards a waymark and metal gate. Go through, cross a track then walk through another metal gate opposite you to the RIGHT. *Look ahead, uphill, and you can make out Llan Ffestiniog church.* Continue uphill, passing waymarks and the

6 This time, however, cross the main road before Meirion House and turn LEFT through a metal gate. Walk past the church and bear RIGHT up some steps to arrive at one of the most spectacular viewpoints in the area. *You can look back over the Cynfal valley to the Rhinog mountains to the south. To the west you can see down the Dwyryd valley to Cardigan Bay, with the Moelwyn mountains dominating the landscape. And, to the north, is Blaenau Ffestiniog with its dramatic slate workings. A picnic table is provided for visitors.* From here return to the starting point.

WALK 18

PANTLLWYD & THE CYNFAL GORGE

DESCRIPTION This 3½ mile walk takes you high above Llan Ffestiniog before descending to cross the Afon Cynfal on a remote footbridge near spectacular waterfalls. Allow 3½ hours.
START Y Pengwern community pub in Llan Ffestiniog square (SH700419).
DIRECTIONS Llan Ffestiniog can be reached from Dolgellau via the A470, Porthmadog via the A487/A496/B4391 and Betws y Coed via the A5/A470. Park in the square in the centre of the village adjoining Y Pengwern pub.
BUS Y TRAIN SERVICES Buses 35 (from Blaenau Ffestiniog and Dolgellau) and 1B (from Blaenau Ffestiniog and Porthmadog) stop at Y Pengwern pub in Llan Ffestiniog. Bus X1 (from Llandudno and Betws y Coed) serves Blaenau Ffestiniog. The town is also served by mainline trains from Llandudno and Betws y Coed, and by Ffestiniog Railway trains from Porthmadog.

1 With your back to the Pengwern pub walk LEFT onto the pavement to the left of the A470. Carefully cross the road and walk up steps past the village war memorial. Turn LEFT, walk uphill and turn LEFT opposite the village shop. Then follow a path RIGHT towards a playground. Ignore paths going left and walk past the playground onto a road. Continue to a junction and turn LEFT downhill to a junction with the A470. Go RIGHT onto the pavement, walk through a lay-by and turn RIGHT onto a minor road. Go RIGHT at a junction and over a railway bridge. *This line ran between Blaenau Ffestiniog and Bala.* Continue uphill to a junction with a main road. Cross, turn LEFT and pass a post-box. Walk RIGHT uphill, over a junction, past a waymark and through a kissing-gate.

2 Continue AHEAD, then bear RIGHT to cross a waymarked stile. Walk AHEAD then, ignoring a path going left, go through a waymarked metal gate to the RIGHT. Go LEFT uphill alongside a wall and old track, then through two wooden gates (the second with a waymark on the adjoining tree). Continue uphill then bear LEFT through a third wooden gate. Bear RIGHT, walking alongside a wall. *The dome-shaped mountain to the LEFT is Manod Mawr.* Ignore a metal gate and rough stile in the wall and continue AHEAD, with the wall now replaced by a fence. Ignore another metal gate, then make for a kissing-gate, crossing a stream just before it. *There are good views from here of the Rhinog mountains to the south-west.*

3 Walk through and AHEAD on a bank above the low wall on your right. Go RIGHT through a gateway and LEFT, following an old track downhill through a metal gate. Walk AHEAD downhill, then across a stream and through another metal gate. Walk to the RIGHT of some sheep pens, passing two gates. Go LEFT through a gateway, then downhill alongside a stream to a metal gate near a road. Go through, then RIGHT past Tyddyn Gwyn Bach house. Continue past a 'Give way' sign, then through an industrial site to the A470. Carefully cross this road and walk LEFT over Bont Newydd, a bridge over the Afon Cynfal. *This river is well-known for its waterfalls and gorge.* Go RIGHT at the end of the bridge and pass Glan Cynfal house. Take the next RIGHT and walk to a waymark.

Stages **4a** *and* **4b** *offer alternative routes to the Cynfal footbridge crossed during Stage 5.* **4a** *follows a path which is occasionally slippery and skirts steep drops. The path is not suitable for children, nor for other inexperienced walkers.* **4b** *follows a minor road and field path, provides open views and takes walkers past an historic farmhouse.*

4a Turn RIGHT at the waymark and follow the path up steps and then alongside the river. *(Given a choice of paths it's best to **bear LEFT** so as to avoid getting too close to the gorge. The main path often uses steps and handrails are provided on occasion).* Soon cross a stream and continue

WALK 18

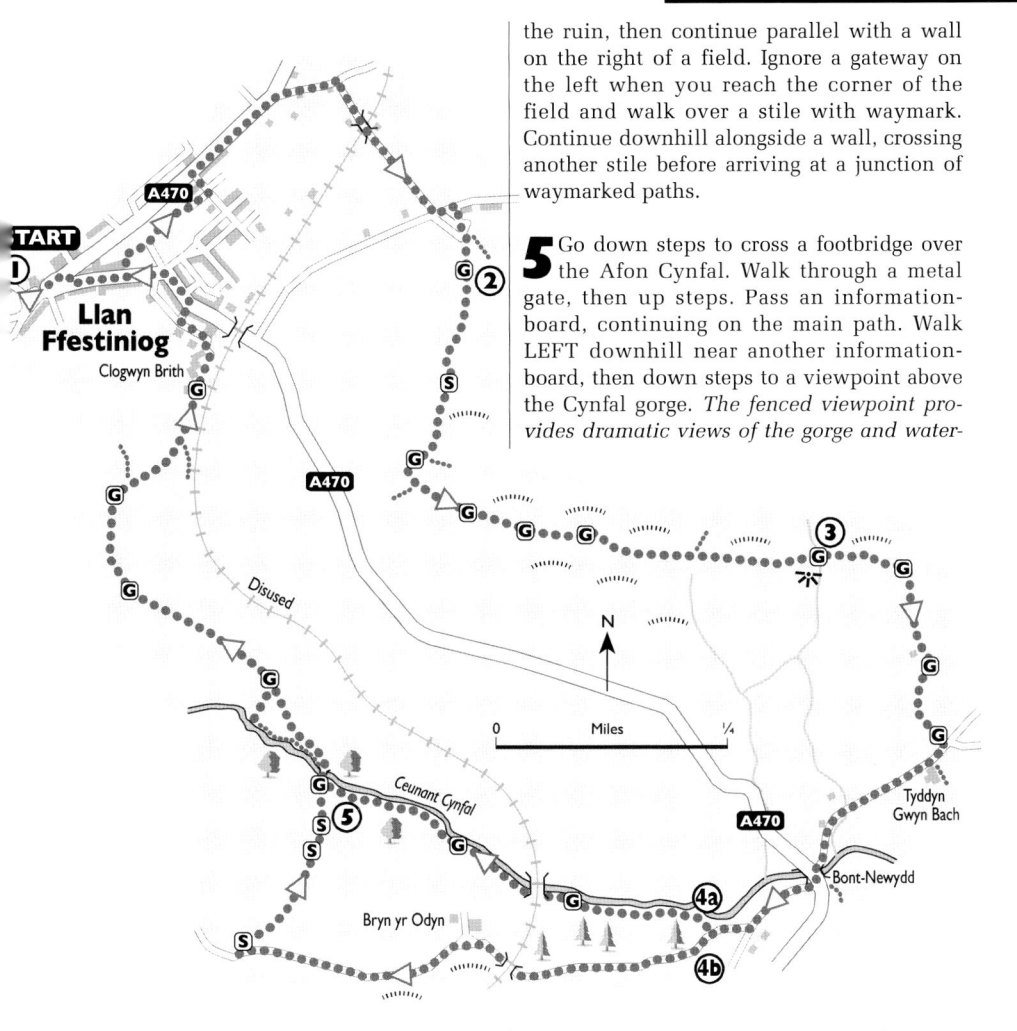

the ruin, then continue parallel with a wall on the right of a field. Ignore a gateway on the left when you reach the corner of the field and walk over a stile with waymark. Continue downhill alongside a wall, crossing another stile before arriving at a junction of waymarked paths.

5 Go down steps to cross a footbridge over the Afon Cynfal. Walk through a metal gate, then up steps. Pass an information-board, continuing on the main path. Walk LEFT downhill near another information-board, then down steps to a viewpoint above the Cynfal gorge. *The fenced viewpoint provides dramatic views of the gorge and water- falls.* Return to the upper path, walk LEFT past the information-board then through a wooden gate. Cross a stream, ignore a path going right and go through a metal gate. Walk uphill, then through a waymarked metal gate. Ignore a path going left and bear RIGHT, following a track uphill. Ignore field gates and a path going right, then go through another metal gate. Follow a road uphill, then take the first road LEFT. Walk downhill past Llan Ffestiniog school, then RIGHT alongside the school entrance. At the A470 turn LEFT and follow the road back to the starting point.

through a wooden gate and beneath a viaduct. *(This carried the Blaenau Ffestiniog to Bala railway line).* Cross another stream and go through another wooden gate. Then walk past a waymark to a junction of waymarked paths.

4b Continue along the road, over a railway bridge *(the Blaenau Ffestiniog to Bala line again)*, then past a barn and house (on the right). *The house, Bryn yr Odyn, dates from about 1550.* Walk past a ruined barn (on the right) to a waymark. Go RIGHT over a stile. Bear RIGHT, walk behind

WALK 19
TEILIAU ISAF & CAECANOL MAWR

DESCRIPTION A 4 mile walk which takes you up the Teigl Valley to an ancient settlement high on the slopes of Manod Mawr mountain. From here there are wonderful views over Llan Ffestiniog to the Dwyryd estuary. Allow 4 hours.
START Y Pengwern community pub in Llan Ffestiniog square (SH700419).
DIRECTIONS Llan Ffestiniog can be reached from Dolgellau via the A470, Porthmadog via the A487/A496/B4391 and Betws y Coed via the A5/A470. Park in the square in the centre of the village adjoining Y Pengwern pub.
BUS & TRAIN SERVICES Buses 35 (from Blaenau Ffestiniog and Dolgellau) and 1B (from Blaenau Ffestiniog and Porthmadog) stop at the Pengwern pub in Llan Ffestiniog. Bus X1 (from Llandudno and Betws y Coed) serves Blaenau Ffestiniog. The town is also served by mainline trains from Llandudno and Betws y Coed, and by Ffestiniog Railway trains from Porthmadog.

1 With your back to the Pengwern pub walk LEFT and join the pavement on the left of the A470. Carefully cross the road and walk up steps past the village war memorial. Turn LEFT, walk uphill and turn LEFT opposite the village shop. Then follow a path RIGHT towards a playground. Ignore paths going left and walk past the playground onto a road. Continue to a junction and turn LEFT downhill to a junction with the A470. Cross the main road and turn RIGHT, passing a bus-stop.

2 Take the first road LEFT and walk downhill. At a junction bear RIGHT, passing a gate to the large house on the left. *This is called Blaen Ddol and is 250 years old.* Ignore a waymark pointing left then go through a metal gate past another waymark. Bear RIGHT at the next junction and go through a wooden gate. *The road going left is to Cae'r Blaidd, now an hotel.*

It dates from 1879. Continue past the hotel and an outbuilding, then through a wooden gate with waymark. Walk downhill, cross a stream then continue past a terrace of houses. Walk across the Afon Teigl and uphill to a road and waymark.

3 Turn LEFT then RIGHT, following a road uphill past a track going right. *This leads to Teiliau Isaf. The farm shares the name Teiliau with two other settlements which you'll pass.* Continue to a main road. Carefully cross this and turn RIGHT. Take the first road LEFT. Go LEFT across a cattle-grid and on a track through a wooden gate. Ignore a right turn and continue uphill until the track levels off. *Half-left here are the mountain peaks of Manod Bach (on the left) and Manod Mawr (right).* Walk through a gateway alongside Teiliau Bach, go RIGHT behind the farmhouse then LEFT alongside the original, much older, house.

4 Follow the track to a wooden gate and walk through the metal gate alongside it. *You are now at a level-crossing on the old Blaenau Ffestiniog to Bala railway line, which closed to passenger trains in 1961.*

WALK 19

Teiliau Bach had its own halt and the farmer travelled to school by train from there during the 1940s. Once over the crossing, pass a track going right and walk uphill alongside a fence. Ignoring a track going left, walk towards a wall and through a metal gate. Continue HALF-RIGHT towards a house. Bear RIGHT and follow a track past the house to a junction. Turn LEFT, passing a waymark and barns. *The settlement to the right is Teiliau Mawr.* Walk RIGHT past a waymark and uphill through three metal gates. Continue past a converted barn and through a gateway. Follow the track LEFT to a metal gate. *This is the entrance to Caecanol Mawr. The house dates from the early 17thC and was built in a commanding position below the cliffs of Manod Mawr. According to legend, the enormous boulder near the house was placed there by the giant Trwsgwl, after he'd removed it from his boot when he was hiking nearby.*

5 Return along the track which bears RIGHT. Then, just before the gateway and the rebuilt barn you passed earlier, turn LEFT through a gap in the wall. Initially, make for the group of trees AHEAD, then bear LEFT, following an old track downhill towards some sheep pens and a ruin. Walk to the RIGHT of the outer boundary wall of the ruin. Then go RIGHT downhill and through a gap in a wall. Bear HALF-LEFT towards a fence. Then go HALF-RIGHT, towards the point where the fence meets another fence at right-angles. To the RIGHT of this point there's a stile. Cross this and then the Teigl river, using an old slate bridge. Continue AHEAD, following a faint path up a grassy slope. This soon levels off and you arrive at a road.

6 Ignore a track going right but turn RIGHT onto the road. Walk past a gated track going left. *This leads to Hafod Yspytty, another ancient settlement.* Ignore a waymark and continue downhill, going through a metal gate alongside a cattle-grid. Cross the Teigl for the third time, ignore waymarks pointing left and right, then go through a gateway. Soon, bear LEFT at a road junction, going through a metal gate alongside another cattle-grid. Pass a converted chapel. *Look half-right to see the Moelwyn mountains (from left to right, Moelwyn Bach, Moelwyn Mawr and Moel yr Hydd).* Ignore waymarks pointing left and right, then cross a bridge before passing another converted chapel. *Built in 1784, this was the first Methodist chapel in the area.* Ignore more waymarks before walking under a railway bridge and continuing past a road going left. Soon go LEFT through a lay-by then continue on a footpath alongside the A470. Turn LEFT just after a bus-stop and return to the starting point.

WALK 20
THE TEIGL RIVER & COED PENGWERN

DESCRIPTION This 3 mile walk offers a variety of unforgettable experiences including splendid mountain views, dramatic waterfalls and unspoilt forest. In addition you will pass several of Llan Ffestiniog's most historically significant settlements. Allow 3½ hours.

START Y Pengwern community pub in Llan Ffestiniog square (SH700419).

DIRECTIONS Llan Ffestiniog can be reached from Dolgellau via the A470, Porthmadog via the A487/A496/B4391 and Betws y Coed via the A5/A470. Park in the square in the centre of the village adjoining Y Pengwern pub.

BUS & TRAIN SERVICES Buses 35 (from Blaenau Ffestiniog and Dolgellau) and 1B (from Blaenau Ffestiniog and Porthmadog) stop at the Pengwern pub in Llan Ffestiniog. Bus X1 (from Llandudno and Betws y Coed) serves Blaenau Ffestiniog. The town is also served by mainline trains from Llandudno and Betws y Coed, and by Ffestiniog Railway trains from Porthmadog.

1 Walk to the LEFT of the Pengwern pub and follow Ty'n y Maes downhill passing roads to left and right. *Look right for a view of Manod Mawr, the dome-shaped mountain to the east of Llan Ffestiniog.* At the end of the terrace of houses go RIGHT past a gated entrance. Walk LEFT, across a stile next to waymarks, then LEFT downhill near a fence on the left of a field. *The mountains to the left are the Moelwyn range. Notice the slate fence alongside you, typical of the region.* Pass a waymark, then cross a stream and stile, next to a gate and waymark, and turn LEFT. Continue downhill between fences, then through a wooden gate with waymark. Pass another waymark and gates to left and right. Walk through a kissing-gate and over another stile with waymark. Go LEFT, following a track downhill. Cross another stile with waymark and continue to a junction of tracks. *The settlement beyond the gate on the left is Plas Meini. This house was built in 1876 for a slate quarry owner. Its garden was designed by Clough Williams-Ellis of Portmeirion fame.*

2 Continue AHEAD, ignoring tracks to left and right, going HALF-RIGHT then LEFT downhill. Ignore a wooden gate on the right before arriving at a metal gate and waymark. Go RIGHT through the gate and down steps, then downhill between walls. At a junction of paths ignore the waymark pointing left and go RIGHT alongside a wall. *Note the carved plaque set in the wall. It is dated 1774 and the letters PM refer to the boundary of the Plas Meini estate.* Walk LEFT past a ruined barn and waymark, and continue to a kissing-gate. Go through, downhill, and across a gated footbridge over the Afon Teigl into Coed Pengwern. *The Teigl flows from high on Manod Mawr and has many spectacular waterfalls.*

3 Walk to the notice-board about Pengwern forest. Continue to the LEFT of it and follow a path alongside the river to a bridge and waymarks. *The forest adjoins Pengwern Old Hall, an important Llan Ffestiniog settlement, after which Y Pengwern pub in the village is named. The forest is ancient woodland which has survived due partly to its inaccessibility.* Turn RIGHT just before the bridge and walk uphill. Ignore a path going left and continue high above the Teigl Gorge. The path descends, levels off, then goes over a stream and up some steps. Soon the path goes down again, alongside a ravine on the left, then uphill to a junction.

4 Here go RIGHT, steeply uphill then LEFT to a stile. Cross and turn LEFT, following a path initially alongside a fence. Bear RIGHT and go through a metal gate. Go AHEAD then bear LEFT uphill to a kissing-gate and waymarks. Walk through then turn RIGHT (not left as indicated) and walk between walls. Go LEFT over a stile at a waymark and uphill alongside the Teigl. *Soon look RIGHT over the river and you'll see a house high above the gorge. This is Cae'r Blaidd, which you'll pass later.*

WALK 20

5 Cross a stream, then a stile and another stream. Walk over another stile, then up several sets of steps and through a wooden gate. Continue uphill, ignoring gates to the house on the right. Go AHEAD through a metal gate with waymark. Turn RIGHT onto the road beyond, then RIGHT again at a waymark. Walk over a bridge and follow a track uphill past a terrace of houses on the left. Cross a stream then go uphill and through a wooden gate with waymark. Follow the track past an outbuilding and Cae'r Blaidd, then walk through another wooden gate and past the driveway to the house. *This dates from 1879 and is now an hotel.* Continue on the tarmac road past a waymark and through a metal gate.

6 Ignore a waymark pointing right then pass a gate into a house on the right. *This is another imposing mansion. It's called Blaen Ddol and is 250 years old.* Continue past the entrance to the house, bearing LEFT and walking uphill to a main road (the A470). Turn RIGHT and walk along the right-hand pavement past a bus-stop. Carefully cross the road here, bear RIGHT then go LEFT onto a road going uphill. Take the first road on the RIGHT and follow it uphill. Join a footpath going AHEAD past a playground. *There are good views here of the Moelwyn mountains (right) and the Lleyn Peninsula (ahead).* Ignore paths going right, then bear LEFT to the A470 and then RIGHT onto the right-hand pavement. Walk downhill then RIGHT down steps alongside Llan Ffestiniog war memorial. Cross the A470, then turn LEFT to return to Y Pengwern pub.

PRONUNCIATION

Welsh	English equivalent
c	always hard, as in **c**at
ch	as in the Scottish word lo**ch**
dd	as th in **th**en
f	as f in o**f**
ff	as ff in o**ff**
g	always hard as in **g**ot
ll	no real equivalent. It is like 'th' in then, but with an 'L' sound added to it, giving 'thlan' for the pronunciation of the Welsh 'Llan'.

In Welsh the accent usually falls on the last-but-one syllable of a word.

KEY TO THE MAPS

- **A470** Main road
- Minor road
- Walk route and direction
- Adjoining path
- Ⓖ Ⓢ Gate/stile
- ② Refer to text instruction
- River/stream
- Trees/woodland
- Railway line
- Disused railway line
- Viewpoint
- Station/buses

THE COUNTRYSIDE CODE

- Be safe – plan ahead and follow any signs
- Leave gates and property as you find them
- Protect plants and animals, and take your litter home
- Keep dogs under close control
- Consider other people

Open Access
Some routes cross areas of land where walkers have the legal right of access under The CRoW Act 2000 introduced in May 2005. Access can be subject to restrictions and closure for land management or safety reasons for up to 28 days a year. Details from: www.naturalresourceswales.gov.uk.
Please respect any notices.

About the author, Michael Burnett...

Michael is a musician who has written articles and presented radio programmes about Welsh traditional music. He is also the author of five other Kittiwake guides: The Rhinogs, East of Snowdon, Coed y Brenin, Barmouth Town and Dolgellau Town. His links to Wales go back to his teenage years when he regularly stayed with friends near Maentwrog and to the 1970s when he lived with his wife, Paula, and their two young children at Blaen Myherin, a remote farmhouse above Devil's Bridge which has now, sadly, become a ruin. Today Michael and Paula share an old farmhouse near the northern Rhinog ridge.

Published by **Kittiwake-Books Limited**
3 Glantwymyn Village Workshops, Glantwymyn,
Machynlleth, Montgomeryshire SY20 8LY

© Text & map research: Michael Burnett 2017
© Maps & illustrations: Kittiwake-Books Ltd 2017

Cover photos: Main: *Manod Mawr from above Bron Manod.* Inset: *Ty Uncorn.* © Michael Burnett 2017.

Care has been taken to be accurate. However neither the author nor the publisher can accept responsibility for any errors which may appear, or their consequences. If you are in any doubt about access, check before you proceed.

Printed by Mixam UK

ISBN: **978 1 908748 46 1**